ELEGANT
ONE-PAN CAKES

ELEGANT
ONE-PAN CAKES

60 Effortless Recipes for Stunning Bakes

SONALI GHOSH

Creator of Sugar Et Al

PAGE
PAGE STREET
PUBLISHING CO.

PAGE STREET
PUBLISHING CO.

First published in 2023 by
Page Street Publishing Co.
27 Congress Street, Suite 1511
Salem, MA 01970
www.pagestreetpublishing.com

Distributed by Macmillan, sales in Canada by The Canadian Manda Group.

27   26   25   24   23   1   2   3   4   5

ISBN-13: 978-1-64567-810-6
ISBN-10: 1-64567-810-5

Library of Congress Control Number: 2022952238

Cover and book design by Molly Kate Young for Page Street Publishing Co.
Photography by Sonali Ghosh

Printed and bound in the United States of America

This book is dedicated to my fearless and remarkable mother,
who showed me by her own example that when we face our fears,
nothing is impossible to accomplish.

To my dynamic father, who instilled in me a passion for books.
Thank you for accompanying me to every book fair, not questioning
my expanding library and supporting my reading habits as a child.
For your tremendous foresight, I am grateful.

❧ CONTENTS ❧

INTRODUCTION

Baking a beautiful cake seems intimidating and challenging to many. Often, people associate a cake with multiple layers in a number of pans, a host of tools and equipment, an arsenal of craft and techniques and a lot of perfection. If it looks beautiful, it has to be a lot of work, right? Absolutely not! With *Elegant One-Pan Cakes,* let me show you that baking cakes can actually become an everyday possibility, a pleasant endeavor and a joyful experience.

At the start of my baking journey, I didn't have many resources or tools. My life transformed drastically when I left my successful corporate career behind in India and moved to Australia with my husband. With two sleeping toddlers in our arms and our entire lives packed into nine suitcases and a few pieces of hand luggage, we entered this breathtaking nation that we now proudly call our home.

Years' worth of belongings suddenly become mere tangibles when you immigrate. Everything gets weighed, only to be equated to baggage allowance. Upon weighing, the kids were allowed to take two toys out of the vast collection of toys they owned at the time. Only one baking pan and a tray for me. Later on, that one pan would alter my life and be the reason for my survival and success in an unknown country.

In fact, people are often surprised when I tell them that I baked my first cake 10 years ago, about the same time that I began writing my blog Sugar Et Al. The blog at the time served as a kind of journal where I could share stories about my stay in Australia and record my baking exploits. I had no idea how much success it would have in the long run, eventually becoming a multi-award-winning business.

With the onset of Sugar Et Al, there was no turning back. Baking was magic—it was pure love! To give my creations a magazine-worthy look, I spent countless months teaching myself professional food photography and styling until it became second nature. As a result of the love I received from my followers and my unwavering passion, I was later able to take on recipe development and photography projects for numerous clients, magazines and businesses. My appreciation of challenges also led my to the commercial space—through perseverance, I briefly owned a café-restaurant.

A cake is similar to a blank canvas that we can use our creative energies to paint on, in our own unique styles. Cake baking does not have to be intimidating or an exhaustive process. It's accessible to people of all levels. It doesn't come with the need for special skills like rowing or scuba diving. Baking is unbiased! You may either take the safe route and stick to tried-and-true recipes, or you can experiment wildly. You always get something wonderful as a gift at the end.

From experience, I can say that the greatest approach to get over the early roadblocks is to bake more, experiment more, make more mistakes and figure out how to go past those mistakes. I hope that this book will dispel some of the apprehensions associated with cake baking and replace them with enthusiasm and joy.

Our limitations often force us to fully appreciate the potential of our resources and explore them in different contexts. Ten years ago, with one pan in hand, I was able to create a variety of one-layered cake recipes. They eventually contributed to the success of my blog. What prevents us from being creative with single-layered cakes? We can frost them, glaze them, booze them up, slather them in gorgeous syrups, top them with interesting combinations of crumbles, poached fruit, meringues—you name it!

In fact, a one-layered beauty is easier to produce, manage, store, transport and devour. It entails that you enjoy all the taste without the substantial serving that comes with a stacked cake. People are now increasingly cautious about quantities, calorie counts and how much sugar and fat they consume. A one-pan cake is a win-win, whether you'd like to think of it as "quality over quantity" or moderation in its best form!

In using one pan, by no means are we limiting ourselves to one-dimensional baked cakes. There are cheesecakes, Bavarians, mousse cakes, ice cream cakes and a stunning charlotte recipe in the book.

Although baking was not a popular activity during my growing-up years, experimenting with flavors, particularly spices, came naturally to me ever since I was a teenager. The book explores a few unusual combinations and a few ingredients that I felt deserved more attention in our kitchens. Spices like cardamom and my absolute favorite, fennel seeds, aren't used in baking as much as they should, which is a shame, because not only are they easily accessible, but they contribute beautifully to a cake with the right pairing. Floral and herbal desserts are a wide and relatively untapped gold mine of possibilities, so I've taken the liberty to experiment with those in different elements in a cake. A jar of culinary lavender or a bottle of rose water is a small investment with a long shelf life that can transform the way people view your cake-making skills.

Elegant One-Pan Cakes is for everyone. No matter where you are currently in your baking journey, there is something new to explore. There are cakes where you literally throw everything into a bowl, and others that require a bit of time to create the different elements. Overall, I have gone to great lengths to simplify every recipe for you.

I think this book speaks to everyone who has a dream, even though I wrote it with bakers and creators in mind. Those who believe, dream and think positively. From a banker 12 years ago to personally creating Elton John's Rocketman cake for Paramount Pictures, I am a walking example of the idea that anything is possible if you truly believe in yourself.

Let this book be a guide for the flavors and techniques, but feel free to use your intuition in replacing fruits that are seasonal and spices, herbs and nuts that are available to you. For example, cashews can be replaced by almonds in the Dulce de Leche and Coffee-Glazed Cashew Cake (page 104). Use peaches or plums in the Apricot and Chamomile Cake (page 116) if apricots aren't in season. Who knows, you may discover something new.

All you need is "one" pan and all the magic happens within. Have fun with it!

Sonali

BAKING TIPS, TECHNIQUES AND PAN SIZE CONVERSIONS

While there is plenty of potential for experimentation and to unleash your creativity in baking, consistency is key as a baker. Paying close attention to details, using exact measurements and following a few easy rules can save you a lot of hassle and guarantee delicious results every time.

Mixing: In many of the recipes in this book, the initial step is to cream the butter and sugar; make sure it's well blended, light and fluffy (which will take at least five minutes). After creaming together the butter and sugar, the next ingredient is eggs. To ensure that the contained air in the creamed butter mixture is retained as well as possible, the eggs should be added one at a time, completely mixed in before adding the next. To ensure that all of this mixture is combined, be careful to scrape the bowl's sides.

After incorporating eggs, the next step usually involves flour. At this stage, overmixing is not a good idea. Flour-based cake batters include gluten, which gets firmer and more elastic the more you mix, beat, knead and so on. Fold in the flour if you want the cakes to be light and fluffy. Overmixing can cause air to escape. If your baked items are coming out too tough to enjoy, try being extra judicious with your mixing.

When using an electric mixer, avoid turning it up too high, since you run the danger of overmixing much more than if you patiently wait for everything to come together on low speed.

Movement: For the purpose of layering, cheesecakes, mousse cakes and Bavarians sometimes need to be transferred in and out of the refrigerator several times. To make it simple to move a springform pan into the freezer or refrigerator, place it on a plate or baking sheet.

Don't overfill the pan. This is gold, even if it has already been stated a million times over. Nobody enjoys a cake that has overflowed and has fallen in the middle, not to mention the subsequent cleanup. Between the batter's surface and the top of the cake pan, there should be at least an inch (2.5 cm). I never fill my pans more than two-thirds of the way up. It is recommended to fill sponge cake pans to only half their height, as such cakes rise more than other cakes.

There are three ways to handle the situation if you are forced to overfill your cake pans:

1. Ensure that your pans are collared. Line the sides with parchment paper to at least ½ to 1 inch (1.3 to 2.5 cm) above the pan rim.

2. Scoop some batter out and bake that batter in a muffin tin, using half of the baking time as a reference.

3. Move low and slow. For instance, if your recipe instructs you to bake something at 350°F (177°C) for 30 minutes, you should instead bake it at 325°F (163°C) for 40 minutes. If it isn't done after 40 minutes of baking, bake it for an additional 5 minutes.

Testing for doneness: When checking for doneness, keep in mind that every oven is unique, thus the baking time specified in the recipe might not always be the same as the time required for your particular oven. Doing the skewer test five minutes before the timer goes off will allow you to quickly determine that you don't end up with an overbaked cake.

Secret ingredient: My secret ingredient for giving my baked goods a lovely, delicate flavor is orange zest. Try grating a little orange zest into your batters, frostings, syrups or jams. It never disappoints.

Make a DIY piping bag: If you're working on a baking project that requires decoration and you don't have a piping bag handy, you can probably make do with what you already have. Fill a zip top bag with your desired icing or frosting and then snip off a corner to your liking.

Baking pans: You'll notice that the majority of the recipes in this book, if not all of them, call for 3-inch (7.5-cm)-deep pans, available in baking supply shops and online. This was intentional. Since they are single-layered cakes, a tall pan provides plenty of room for the cake to rise and take on a lovely form. Due to its high edges, it offers greater protection to your batter in the oven, resulting in a finished cake that is lighter in color and moister. Additionally, a cake with height appears elegant and professional.

Pan size conversions: While it's always advised to follow a recipe exactly, there are times when adjustments are needed because you don't have the appropriate pan size. In these situations, a little math can help. By modifying the baking time, you may use the same recipe or cake mix with confidence.

The easiest method is by finding out the surface area in square inches of the pan you're asked to use vs. the one you own. Typically, if this is within 10 percent of each other, there is no need to adjust the baking time. For example, if your recipe calls for baking in a 9-inch (23-cm) round pan (64 square inches [413 square cm]) and you own an 8-inch (20-cm) square pan (50 square inches [323 square cm]) there is no need to adjust the baking time.

Formulas for calculating your own:

- Square or rectangular pan: Area = length × width
- Round pan: Area = (½ its diameter)^2 × 3.14

If you're transferring the recipe to a smaller pan and the batter looks too deep, reduce the oven temperature by 25°F (4°C) and lengthen the baking time by a quarter of the original time stated in the recipe. Increase the oven temperature by 25°F (4°C) and shorten the baking time by a quarter of the original time stated in the recipe if you're transferring the recipe to a bigger pan. The cake will still come out thinner, but the flavor and texture should be all right. In either case, it is ideal to begin checking for doneness 10 minutes before the new estimated time.

How to modify the pan size if the batch size changes: If you double or halve a recipe, the idea stays the same. Make sure you choose the correct pans and adjust the temperatures accordingly. If you wish to double a recipe, for instance, you should choose a pan that is roughly double the area of the original pan or use two of the recommended size pans. Otherwise, you will need to change the baking time to make up the difference.

Another key thing to remember is that weighing ingredients, especially when using metric measures, makes it simpler to scale up or down a recipe. While measuring by volume is straightforward, splitting a measurement like ¾ cup in half takes a little more work. According to the metric system, a recipe that asks for ⅔ cup of granulated sugar is 133 g, therefore cutting it in half rounds to 67 g. More sensible!

CACAO THERAPY

Cacao, cocoa or chocolate! It's not a name, it is an emotion. It is the most effective and affordable therapy we can have. I wonder if it would be easier to handle stress if it were coated in chocolate.

A favorite treat, a childhood memory, a romantic ritual, a quick fix on a bad day, life's greatest pleasure on certain days and a superfood with antioxidants and anti-inflammatory characteristics on other days. Almost nothing about chocolate hasn't been written about previously. So, the only thing I'm going to say is that Cacao Therapy is an excuse to expand your chocolate horizons.

I think the best way to celebrate the versatility of chocolate is to experiment with a flavor combination you've never tried before. Push the envelope if you're a seasoned chocolate fan by combining it with tangy rhubarb, zesty blood oranges, tahini, sea salt or olive oil. Chocolate is a universal component that works well with both tea and coffee. With the Chocolate Earl Grey Mousse Cake (page 29) and Mocha Flan (page 38), I've got both covered for you.

For the purists, I have the classic Chocolate, Hazelnut and Raspberry Cake (page 22) and a gluten-free Dark Chocolate, Orange and Pecan Torte featuring everyone's favorite pairing, chocolate and orange (page 33). If you're like me and love visualizing everything in cake form, you're going to love the Aussie Lamington Cake (page 34) all the way from Down Under.

The only real question you need to ask yourself is, "Which of these delectable chocolate cakes do I want to try first?"

CARAMEL CAKE WITH SALTED CHOCOLATE FROSTING

≫ Makes an 8-inch (20-cm) round cake ≪

Beautiful to behold, this rich golden caramel cake, topped with velvety peaks of chocolate fudge frosting and a smattering of sea salt, is not for the fainthearted. This is a novel way to play with chocolate and caramel. The soft caramel cake serves as the ideal base, while adding salt to chocolate enhances its flavor and mutes its bitterness.

Caramel Cake

Canola oil spray, for pan

½ cup (114 g) unsalted butter, at room temperature

¾ cup (165 g) light or dark brown sugar

2 tbsp (30 ml) golden syrup or honey

2 large eggs, at room temperature

1 tsp lemon zest

1½ cups (188 g) self-rising flour

½ cup (51 g) almond meal

½ cup (120 ml) buttermilk

Chocolate Fudge Frosting

4 oz (115 g) dark chocolate, chopped roughly

⅔ cup (152 g) unsalted butter, at room temperature

1⅓ cups (160 g) powdered sugar, sifted

For Assembly

1 oz (28 g) dark chocolate, shaved with a peeler

1 tsp flaky sea salt

Make the caramel cake: Preheat the oven to 350°F (177°C). Spray the base and sides of an 8-inch (20-cm) round, 3-inch (8-cm)-deep cake pan with canola oil and line the base with parchment paper.

In a large bowl, beat together the butter, brown sugar and golden syrup until pale and fluffy. Add the eggs, one at a time, beating well after each addition. Beat in the lemon zest. Fold in the flour and almond meal, alternately with the buttermilk, until just combined.

Transfer the mixture to the prepared pan. Bake for 45 to 55 minutes, or until a skewer inserted into the middle of the cake comes out clean. Remove the cake from the oven. Set it aside for 5 minutes, then carefully turn it out onto a wire rack to cool completely before frosting.

Make the chocolate fudge frosting: Place the chocolate in a heatproof bowl. Melt the chocolate by placing the bowl atop a saucepan of simmering water (make sure the bottom of the bowl doesn't touch the water). Remove from the heat and allow to cool to room temperature.

In a medium-sized bowl, using an electric mixer, beat the butter until smooth, about 1 minute. Add the powdered sugar and beat until light and fluffy, about 2 minutes. Add the melted chocolate and beat on low speed until well combined. Increase the speed to medium-high and continue to beat until the frosting looks smooth and glossy, about 2 minutes.

Assemble: Once the cake has cooled to room temperature, transfer the frosting to a piping bag fitted with a large round tip. Starting from the edges, pipe frosting kisses all over the top of the cake, leaving a small gap in the center for the chocolate shavings. Sprinkle the top with sea salt and chocolate shavings.

CHOCOLATE, HAZELNUT AND RASPBERRY CAKE

⇛ Makes a 7-inch (18-cm) round cake ⇚

Believe it or not, even though this absolutely stunning cake looks like something you'd buy at a fancy, upscale bakery, the ingredients are simply thrown into a saucepan. And if you think it looks amazing, just wait till you try a mouthful.

Chocolate, Hazelnut and Raspberry Cake

Canola oil spray, for pan

¾ cup (170 g) unsalted butter, at room temperature

1½ cups (330 g) light or dark brown sugar

¾ cup (180 ml) milk

½ cup (44 g) unsweetened cocoa powder

½ tsp baking soda

1 cup (125 g) self-rising flour

¼ cup (51 g) hazelnut meal (ground hazelnuts)

3 large eggs, whisked lightly

½ cup (62 g) raspberries, fresh or frozen

Chocolate Hazelnut Frosting

¼ cup (57 g) unsalted butter, at room temperature

⅓ cup (about 100 g) chocolate hazelnut spread

1 cup (120 g) powdered sugar

1 tbsp (15 ml) heavy cream

For Assembly

2 oz (50 g) dark chocolate, grated

½ cup (62 g) fresh raspberries, for garnish

Make the chocolate, hazelnut and raspberry cake: Preheat the oven to 350°F (177°C). Spray the base and sides of a 7-inch (18-cm) round, 3-inch (7.5-cm)-deep cake pan with canola oil and line the base with parchment paper.

In a large saucepan, combine the butter, brown sugar, milk, cocoa powder and baking soda, and cook over low heat until the butter has melted and the mixture is smooth. Remove the pan from the heat and set it aside for 15 minutes to cool.

Fold in the flour and hazelnut meal, and mix. Add the whisked eggs and mix till incorporated. Fold in the raspberries.

Pour the mixture into the prepared pan. Bake for 75 to 80 minutes, or until a skewer inserted into the middle of the cake comes out clean. Remove the cake from the oven. Set it aside for 10 minutes, then gently run a blunt knife around the edges to loosen the cake. Carefully turn it out onto a wire rack to cool completely.

Make the frosting: In a medium-sized bowl, using an electric mixer on low speed, beat the butter until light and fluffy. Add the chocolate hazelnut spread and continue to beat until incorporated.

Add the powdered sugar, a little a time, beating constantly, until well combined, scraping down the sides of the bowl as needed. Add the cream and beat on medium-high speed until the frosting is light and fluffy, about 2 minutes.

Assemble: Using a piping bag fitted with an open star tip, pipe the chocolate hazelnut frosting onto the top of the cake. Spread a thin layer of frosting on the sides. Decorate the sides with grated chocolate by using the palm of your hand to gently press the shavings onto the frosting. Decorate the top with of the cake with fresh raspberries.

BLOOD ORANGE CHOCOLATE UPSIDE-DOWN CAKE

≫ Makes an 8-inch (20-cm) round cake ≪

In my humble opinion, the greatest citrus that will ever be are blood oranges. Utilize their inherent theatrical abilities and let them play the lead role in this lovely chocolate cake. The cake has a zesty flavor of blood orange zest and juice and is rich, nutty and aromatic.

Blood Orange Topping

Canola oil spray, for pan

3 tbsp (43 g) unsalted butter

½ cup (100 g) granulated sugar

3 medium-sized blood oranges, sliced ¼" (6 mm) thick

Blood Orange Chocolate Cake

½ cup + 1 tbsp (126 g) unsalted butter, chopped roughly

1 cup (220 g) light or dark brown sugar

3 large eggs

¾ cup (94 g) all-purpose flour

⅓ cup (41 g) self-rising flour

½ cup (51 g) almond meal

¼ cup (22 g) unsweetened cocoa powder

½ tsp baking soda

1 tbsp (6 g) fresh blood orange zest

⅓ cup (80 ml) sour cream

¼ cup (60 ml) blood orange juice

Make the blood orange topping: Preheat the oven to 325°F (163°C). Spray the base and sides of an 8-inch (20-cm) round, 3-inch (8-cm)-deep cake pan with canola oil and line the base with parchment paper.

Place the butter in the prepared cake pan and place the pan in the oven to melt the butter, about 2 minutes. Using a pastry brush, spread the butter evenly to cover the base of the pan. Sprinkle the granulated sugar evenly over the butter. Starting from the center, layer the orange slices on top of the sugar, overlapping them in a spiral pattern. Set the pan aside while you make the cake batter.

Make the blood orange chocolate cake: In a large bowl, beat together the butter and brown sugar until pale and creamy. Add the eggs, one at a time, beating well after each addition.

Add the all-purpose and self-rising flours, almond meal, cocoa powder, baking soda and blood orange zest, folding the mixture to combine. Add the sour cream and blood orange juice. Fold again until just combined.

Spread the mixture over the orange topping in the cake pan and smooth the surface. Bake for 65 to 75 minutes, or until a skewer inserted into the center comes out clean. Remove from the oven. Set aside in the pan for 15 minutes to cool slightly before turning out onto a serving plate. Slice and serve.

CHOCOLATE AND RHUBARB CAKE

A little goes a long way for this richly satisfying cake. Tangy rhubarb is a great match for rich chocolate, and together they are a sensation. The creamy chocolate cream cheese frosting ties them together perfectly for a tasty explosion.

Rhubarb Compote

8 rhubarb stalks (about 10 oz [300 g]), trimmed and chopped

½ cup (120 ml) water

½ cup (100 g) granulated sugar

1 tsp vanilla extract

Chocolate Cake

Canola oil spray, for pan

¼ cup (31 g) all-purpose flour

¼ cup (31 g) self-rising flour

¼ tsp baking soda

¼ cup (22 g) unsweetened cocoa powder

½ cup (114 g) unsalted butter, chopped roughly

3.5 oz (100 g) dark chocolate

¾ cup (150 g) granulated sugar

2 medium-sized eggs

¾ cup (180 ml) buttermilk

Chocolate Cream Cheese Frosting

4 oz (115 g) cream cheese, at room temperature

¼ cup (57 g) unsalted butter, at room temperature

1½ cups (180 g) powdered sugar

2 tbsp (11 g) Dutch-processed cocoa powder

Make the rhubarb compote: This can be done the night before, just prior to making the cake or while the cake is baking. In a medium-sized saucepan, combine the rhubarb, water and granulated sugar. Cook over medium-high heat until the rhubarb breaks down and the mixture is thick, 7 to 8 minutes.

Remove the saucepan from the heat. Add the vanilla. Stir and allow the mixture to cool to room temperature. Store in the refrigerator until needed.

Make the chocolate cake: Preheat the oven to 350°F (177°C). Spray the base and sides of a 7-inch (18-cm) round, 3-inch (8-cm)-deep cake pan with canola oil and line the base with parchment paper.

In a large bowl, stir together the all-purpose and self-rising flours, baking soda and cocoa powder.

In a medium-sized saucepan, combine the butter, chocolate and granulated sugar. Cook, stirring, over low heat, until the butter has melted and the mixture is smooth, about 5 minutes. Set aside to cool.

In a separate medium-sized bowl, whisk together the eggs and buttermilk.

Stir the chocolate mixture and the buttermilk mixture alternately into the flour mixture. Pour half of the batter into the prepared cake pan. Spread with 4 tablespoons (90 g) of the rhubarb compote. Pour the rest of the batter over the rhubarb compote and spread evenly.

Bake for 55 to 65 minutes, or until a skewer inserted into the middle of the cake comes out clean. Remove the cake from the oven and allow to rest in the pan for 10 minutes. Gently turn the cake out onto a wire rack to cool.

Make the chocolate cream cheese frosting: Using a medium-sized bowl and an electric mixer, beat the cream cheese and the butter together until smooth and creamy. Add the powdered sugar, ½ cup (60 g) at a time, beating after each addition until smooth. Add the cocoa powder and beat till well blended.

Assemble: Place the cooled cake on a cake stand or plate. Transfer the frosting to a piping bag fitted with an open star tip. Pipe swirls to form a border around the cake. Spoon 4 tablespoons (90 g) of the rhubarb compote in the center. Slice the cake and serve.

CHOCOLATE EARL GREY MOUSSE CAKE

Although there is an art to brewing the perfect cup of tea, no particular talents are needed to make this delectable mousse cake. Neither gelatin nor eggs are necessary for the mousse. The highlight of the mousse cake is the tea of course! Earl Grey tea is so alluring and memorable because of its bergamot undertone. Paired with chocolate, it is nothing short of phenomenal. You will need a moment alone to savor this one.

Cookie Crust

Canola oil spray, for pan

14 to 15 chocolate cookies (160 g)

⅓ cup (76 g) unsalted butter, melted

Mousse Filling

2½ cups (600 ml) heavy cream, divided

2 Earl Grey tea bags

14 oz (400 g) dark chocolate, chopped roughly

Chocolate Glaze

2.5 oz (70 g) dark chocolate, chopped roughly

¼ cup (60 ml) heavy cream

1 tbsp (15 ml) liquid glucose or light corn syrup

For Assembly

1 cup (140 g) fresh berries

4 figs (160 g), quartered

Make the cookie crust: Spray the base and sides of an 8-inch (20-cm) round springform pan with canola oil and line the base with parchment paper. In a food processor, process the cookies until they resemble fine crumbs. Add the butter and process briefly until combined. Press the cookie mixture evenly onto the base of the prepared pan. Chill in the fridge for 30 minutes.

Make the mousse filling: In a small saucepan, heat ½ cup (120 ml) of the cream over low heat. When the cream is about to steam (do not boil), remove from the heat and place the tea bags in the cream to infuse. Set the mixture aside to cool while frequently pressing the tea bags with the back of a spoon to extract maximum tea flavor.

Place the chocolate in a large heatproof bowl over a saucepan of simmering water (do not let the bowl touch the water). Stir with a metal spoon for 10 minutes, or until melted and smooth. Remove the chocolate from the heat and allow to cool for 10 to 15 minutes.

In a large bowl, using an electric mixer, beat the remaining 2 cups (480 ml) of cream until soft peaks form. Fold in the tea-infused cream, then fold in the melted chocolate until the filling is smooth.

Pour the chocolate mousse filling over the cookie crust in the prepared pan. Smooth the surface with a spatula, then cover the pan and refrigerate for 3 hours, or until set. When the mousse is set, gently remove the ring from the springform pan.

Make the chocolate glaze: In a small saucepan, combine the chocolate, cream and glucose. Stir the mixture over low heat until melted and smooth. Remove from the heat and let cool slightly. Pour the glaze over the set mousse. Place the mousse cake back in the fridge to set for about an hour.

Assemble: Once the glaze has set and you are ready to serve, decorate the mousse cake with fresh berries and figs. Slice and enjoy cold.

BANANA TAHINI CAKE WITH OLIVE OIL GANACHE

If you can't eat nuts but still want your cake to have a wonderful nutty texture, tahini is a fantastic alternative. The toasted sesame seed flavor from the tahini is what makes this banana cake unique. But what raises it to a new level is the olive oil ganache. A ganache made with olive oil is silkier, smoother and, depending on the type of olive oil used, may have a more upscale flavor. This is the kind of cake that can be made quickly throughout the workweek.

Banana Tahini Cake
Canola oil spray, for pan

¼ cup (57 g) unsalted butter, melted

1 large egg

1 ripe banana, mashed (about ½ cup [115 g])

⅓ cup (73 g) light or dark brown sugar

1 tbsp (15 g) hulled tahini

½ cup (120 ml) milk

1 cup (125 g) self-rising flour

½ tsp baking soda

Olive Oil Ganache
3.5 oz (100 g) dark chocolate, chopped roughly

1 tbsp (15 ml) extra virgin olive oil

1 tsp honey

Make the banana tahini cake: Preheat the oven to 350°F (177°C). Spray the base and sides of a 7-inch (18-cm) round, 3-inch (7.5-cm)-deep cake pan with canola oil and line the base with parchment paper.

In a large bowl, beat together the butter, egg, banana, brown sugar, tahini and milk. Add the flour and baking soda and continue to beat until just combined.

Transfer the batter to the prepared cake pan. Bake for 45 to 50 minutes, or until a skewer inserted into the middle of the cake comes out clean. Remove the cake from the oven. Set it aside for 10 minutes, then gently run a blunt knife around the edges to loosen the cake. Carefully turn it out onto a wire rack to cool completely.

Make the olive oil ganache: In a medium-sized saucepan, combine the chocolate, olive oil and honey. Cook over low heat, stirring frequently, until the chocolate has melted and the ganache looks smooth and glossy, about 5 minutes. Remove the pan from the heat. Set aside for 30 minutes, or until the ganache has thickened and is of a spreadable consistency.

Assemble: Place the cooled cake on a cake plate or stand. Using an offset spatula or the back of a large spoon, spread the ganache over the surface of the cake. Slice and serve.

DARK CHOCOLATE, ORANGE AND PECAN TORTE

≫ Makes an 8-inch (20-cm) round cake ≪

This cake's structure is made up entirely of pecans and chocolate, and it has no flour. Although suited for a gluten-free diet, it is so decadent it will prove to be a hit for everyone. Pecans are known to be heart-healthy and immune system strengthening, while dark chocolate has more antioxidants than most food, so this cake is undoubtedly beneficial for the body, heart and mind.

Canola oil spray, for pan

1 cup (109 g) chopped pecans

½ cup (100 g) + 2 tbsp (30 g) sugar, divided

9 oz (255 g) dark chocolate (see Note), chopped roughly

1 tsp finely grated orange zest

7 large egg whites

½ tsp cream of tartar

For Assembly

½ cup (120 ml) heavy cream, whipped to stiff peaks

1 tbsp (14 g) grated dark chocolate, for garnish

NOTE: The taste of the torte largely depends on the quality of chocolate used. So, it's imperative that you use a good brand of chocolate. You could also use an orange-flavored chocolate and skip the orange zest. It works great! So does any other flavored chocolate.

Preheat the oven to 350°F (177°C). Spray the base and sides of an 8-inch (20-cm) round springform pan with canola oil and line the base with parchment paper.

In a food processor, pulse the pecans with 1 tablespoon (15 g) of the sugar until finely ground. Transfer the nuts to a medium-sized bowl. Wipe the bowl of the food processor with a paper towel to remove any oils that may have appeared while processing the pecans.

In the clean food processor, combine the chopped chocolate with 1 tablespoon (15 g) of the sugar and pulse until the mixture has the consistency of a coarse meal with some small bits (about ¼-inch [6-mm] pieces) of chocolate. Transfer the chocolate and the orange zest to the bowl containing the ground nuts. Set the bowl aside until needed.

In a large bowl, using an electric mixer, beat together the egg whites and cream of tartar on medium speed until the whites start to form soft peaks. Add the remaining ½ cup (100 g) of sugar and increase the speed to medium-high, beating constantly until the egg whites are glossy and stiff.

With a large rubber spatula, fold the nut mixture gradually into the egg whites until well incorporated, taking care not to deflate the egg whites too much.

Transfer the batter to the prepared pan, scraping the sides of the bowl as needed. Bake for 35 minutes, or until the torte is golden brown on the top and a skewer inserted into the middle of the torte comes out stained with melted chocolate but not raw batter. Remove the cake from the oven. Set it aside for 10 minutes, then gently run a blunt knife around the edges and the center to loosen the cake. Carefully remove the ring of the springform pan and place the pan on a wire rack to cool completely.

Assemble: Using a piping bag fitted with an open star nozzle, pipe swirls of the whipped cream onto the torte. Sprinkle grated chocolate over the cream. Slice and serve.

AUSSIE LAMINGTON CAKE

Australia's culinary pleasures are distinctive, fascinating and even a touch quirky! But where they truly shine is in their capacity to bring people together through community gatherings and story sharing.

According to legend, a maid for Queensland governor Lord Lamington mistakenly slipped cake into chocolate sauce. So that his fingers didn't become sticky, the governor ordered that it be rolled in coconut, and that's how the lamington was born. I promise that my easy lamington cake will have you licking your fingers.

Sponge Cake
Canola oil spray, for pan

1 cup (125 g) all-purpose flour

¼ cup (32 g) cornstarch

2 tbsp (28 g) unsalted butter, at room temperature

⅓ cup (80 ml) boiling water

4 large eggs, at room temperature

¾ cup (150 g) granulated sugar

Chocolate Icing
2 cups (240 g) powdered sugar

¼ cup (22 g) unsweetened cocoa powder

1 tbsp (14 g) unsalted butter

⅓ cup (80 ml) milk

For Assembly
1 cup (90 g) desiccated coconut, for sprinkling

Make the sponge cake: Preheat the oven to 350°F (177°C). Spray the base and sides of an 8-inch (20-cm) round, 3-inch (7.5-cm)-deep cake pan with canola oil and line the base with parchment paper.

Into a medium-sized bowl, sift the flour and cornstarch twice. In a small cup or bowl, combine the butter and boiling water. Set both mixtures aside.

In a large bowl, beat the eggs until light and fluffy. Add the granulated sugar and continue to beat until tripled in volume, 7 to 8 minutes. The mixture should look thick and fall back as thick ribbons when the beaters are lifted.

Gently fold the flour mixture into the egg mixture, then fold in the butter mixture. Do this gradually so as to not deflate the batter too much.

Transfer the batter to the prepared pan and smooth out the surface with a spatula. Bake for 37 to 45 minutes, or until the sponge starts to pull away from the sides and springs back when lightly touched.

Remove the pan from the oven. Set it aside for 10 minutes, then gently run a blunt knife around the edges to loosen the cake. Carefully turn it out onto a wire rack to cool completely. Place the cake in the fridge for 30 minutes to firm it up for easy handling.

Make the chocolate icing: In a medium-sized saucepan, combine the powdered sugar, cocoa powder, butter and milk. Bring to a boil over low heat while stirring frequently. Continue to heat until the mixture comes to a simmer and is thick and smooth. Remove from the heat and set aside to cool.

Assemble: Place the sponge cake still on its wire rack, on a large plate (to catch the drips). Spread the chocolate icing all over the top and sides of the cake. Sprinkle the top and sides with desiccated coconut.

CHOCOLATE BISCUIT CAKE

Chocolate biscuit cake was supposedly the late Queen Elizabeth II's favorite dessert. I'm not sure whether Her Majesty would have approved of my streamlined cheat's version, but my two teenage children think it's fantastic. It's super simple and requires no baking.

Biscuit Cake

Canola oil spray, for pan

21 oz (600 g) graham crackers or digestive biscuits, chopped roughly into small pieces

½ cup (72 g) whole mixed nuts (almonds, walnuts, pistachios), roasted

1 cup (240 ml) water

1 cup (200 g) sugar

½ cup (44 g) unsweetened cocoa powder

⅔ cup (152 g) unsalted butter, cubed

Chocolate Ganache

½ cup (120 ml) heavy cream

4 oz (120 g) dark chocolate, chopped into small pieces

1 tbsp (15 ml) glucose syrup or light corn syrup (optional)

1 tsp finely grated orange zest (optional)

For Assembly

Chocolate chips

Make the biscuit cake: Spray the base and sides of a 9-inch (23-cm) round, 3-inch (7.5-cm)-deep cake pan with canola oil and line the base with parchment paper.

In a large bowl, stir together the chopped graham crackers and nuts.

In a medium-sized saucepan, combine the water, sugar, cocoa powder and butter. Cook over low heat, stirring frequently, until the sugar has melted and the mixture is smooth. Remove from the heat and set aside for 15 minutes to cool.

Pour the cocoa mixture over the cookie base. Mix well so all the crumbs and nuts are covered and coated thoroughly.

Pour the mixture into the prepared pan. Use a spatula to gently pack it into an even layer, pressing down if required. Cover the pan with plastic wrap and chill in the refrigerator for at least 2 hours.

Make the chocolate ganache: In a medium-sized microwave-safe bowl, combine the cream and chocolate. Microwave on medium power (50%) for 2 to 3 minutes, removing from the microwave and stirring every 30 seconds with a metal spoon until smooth. Add the glucose syrup and orange zest (if using), and mix until smooth and glossy. Set aside for 5 minutes to cool down slightly.

Assemble: Remove the cake from the fridge. Pour the ganache over the top of the cake. Tilt the pan slightly on all sides so the ganache spreads evenly to the sides to get an even coating. Refrigerate the cake for 2 hours, or until the ganache has completely set. When the cake is ready to serve, decorate with chocolate chips.

Allow the cake to sit at room temperature for at least 30 minutes before slicing into it.

MOCHA FLAN

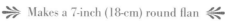 Makes a 7-inch (18-cm) round flan

My husband has a thing for eggs. Like a mother hen, he guards them on the way home from the grocery store. He even has a protective enclosure in his car to keep them from falling over or shifting. Once inside, he is the only one who is authorized to carry the bag until the eggs are secure in the refrigerator. If eggs are also your favorite food, save them for this wonderful custard dessert.

A good flan should have a silky, delicate texture that is creamy and smooth. The sauce must be a deep golden caramel color and completely free of any burnt flavor. This make-ahead flan is certainly evidence of how delicious coffee, caramel and chocolate can coexist in a dessert and is the perfect way to end a memorable dinner!

Caramel
½ cup (100 g) sugar
¼ cup (60 ml) water

Flan
1½ cups (300 ml) heavy cream
¾ cup (180 ml) milk
6 oz (170 g) dark chocolate, chopped roughly
1 tsp instant coffee powder
3 large eggs
3 large egg yolks
¼ cup (50 g) sugar

For Assembly
Edible gold leaf, to decorate (optional)
Fresh berries or cherries, for garnish

Make the caramel: In a small saucepan, combine the sugar and water. Heat over low heat for 2 to 3 minutes, stirring and brushing down the inside of the pan until the sugar dissolves.

Continue to boil without stirring for 5 to 10 minutes, or until the mixture caramelizes. Remove from the heat and allow any bubbles to subside.

Pour the caramel into a 7-inch (18-cm) round, 3-inch (7.5-cm)-deep cake pan, swirling to coat the base of the pan completely. Set the pan aside while you prepare the flan.

Make the flan: Preheat the oven to 325°F (163°C). In a medium-sized saucepan, combine the cream, milk, chocolate and coffee powder. Cook over low heat, stirring frequently, for 3 to 5 minutes, or until smooth. Remove from the heat and set aside to cool slightly.

In a medium-sized bowl, whisk together the eggs, egg yolks and sugar until well combined. Gradually whisk in the cream mixture.

Pour the egg mixture gradually over the caramel layer in the cake pan. Place the cake pan inside a larger pan or baking dish, and pour enough boiling water into the larger pan to come halfway up the sides of the cake pan (this is called creating a bain-marie or water bath).

Bake for 40 to 45 minutes, or until the flan looks almost set. It should be slightly wobbly in the center. Remove the pan from the oven and set aside to cool to room temperature. Chill in the fridge for 3 to 4 hours, or preferably overnight.

Assemble: When ready to serve, run a blunt knife around the edges to loosen the flan. Very carefully invert it onto a serving plate. If desired, decorate with edible gold leaf. Slice and serve with fresh berries or cherries.

AFTERNOON TEA

It is said that Queen Victoria's close companion Anna, the Duchess of Bedford, started the iconic British ritual of afternoon tea in the nineteenth century. What started out as a private affair evolved into a social event that filled the time between lunch and dinner. The success of afternoon tea over time may be attributed to the appeal of tea and the opportunity to socialize. An afternoon tea often includes scones, cakes, sandwiches and freshly brewed tea.

English customs had a big influence on Australian culture throughout the colonial era. One of them was afternoon tea.

When I first came to live in Australia, I was both intrigued and delighted when I was invited to afternoon tea. So, having guests over for tea can be a thing? Furthermore, it had a name. Back when I was growing up in India, people were only invited to lunch or dinner; it would be considered impolite otherwise.

In today's fast-paced world, afternoon tea is more like a break on a busy day, a treat for oneself or a chance to indulge in a slice of cake over short conversations with friends.

Typically, these cakes aren't overly iced or ornamented and are just plain, light and easy to consume. I've included a lot of fruit-based cakes since they make excellent afternoon tea treats. The Cardamom and Rhubarb Cake (page 44) and the Plum and Ginger Crumble Cake (page 48) are both made better by their bit of spice. In addition to an Earl Grey Cake with Strawberry Icing (page 56) that includes strawberries in the glaze for an added boost in flavor and color, there is a Fresh Strawberry Poppy Seed Cake (page 43) prepared from pureed strawberries. The Orange Olive Oil Cake (page 63) is straightforward but energizing, as a lovely citrus cake ought to be. The loaf cakes, must-haves for any afternoon tea, should not be missed.

So, when are you throwing your own afternoon tea party?

FRESH STRAWBERRY POPPY SEED CAKE

My son's first grade teacher taught the class something that they may have forgotten, but it has stuck with me ever since: "If anyone is being mean to you, kill them with your kindness!" Well, kindness comes in all forms. If you have a "meanie" in your life, you may want to present them with this cake. For what better way to show generosity than a beautiful cake made of freshly pureed strawberries, topped with a copious amount of condensed milk buttercream and pretty flowers. Sweet as it should be!

Strawberry Reduction
8 oz (225 g) fresh strawberries

1 tsp fresh lemon juice

Fresh Strawberry Cake
Canola oil spray, for pan

¼ cup (57 g) unsalted butter, melted

¾ cup (150 g) sugar

2 large eggs, whisked lightly

1 cup (125 g) self-rising flour

1 tbsp (8 g) poppy seeds

½ cup (120 ml) strawberry reduction

1 tbsp (15 ml) milk

2 drops pink food coloring (optional)

Strawberry Condensed Milk Frosting
½ cup (114 g) unsalted butter, at room temperature

7 oz (200 g) sweetened condensed milk, at room temperature

1 tbsp (15 ml) strawberry reduction

For Assembly
7 to 8 strawberries, cut into halves and quarters

Edible flowers

Make the strawberry reduction: It's best to do this either the night before or a couple of hours before starting on the cake, so the reduction has time to thicken and cool down.

In a medium-sized saucepan, using a stick blender, blend all the strawberries until they become a smooth puree.

Add the lemon juice and place the saucepan over low heat. Bring to a simmer, increasing the heat to medium while stirring frequently. Cook until the strawberry mixture is reduced by half, 20 to 25 minutes, and resembles tomato paste. You should have about ⅔ cup (160 ml) of the reduction.

Pour the strawberry reduction into a cup. Set aside to cool, then store in the refrigerator until needed. This reduction will be used for both the cake and its frosting.

Make the fresh strawberry cake: Preheat the oven to 350°F (177°C). Spray the base and sides of a 7-inch (18-cm) round, 3-inch (7.5-cm)-deep cake pan with canola oil and line the base with parchment paper.

In a large bowl, combine the butter, sugar, eggs, flour, poppy seeds, strawberry reduction and milk. Beat until well mixed, 2 to 3 minutes, then beat in the food coloring (if using).

Pour the batter into the prepared pan. Smooth the top with the back of a spoon. Bake for 55 to 60 minutes, or until a skewer inserted into the middle of the cake comes out clean. Remove the cake from the oven. Set it aside for 5 minutes, then carefully turn it out onto a wire rack to cool completely before frosting.

Make the frosting: In a medium-sized bowl, beat the butter until light and fluffy, 2 to 3 minutes. Add the condensed milk, a little at a time, and continue to beat until well blended. Add the strawberry reduction and beat until the frosting looks thick and glossy.

Assemble: Once the cake has cooled to room temperature, use an offset spatula or the back of a large spoon to spread the frosting on the top of the cake. Decorate with fresh strawberries and edible flowers.

CARDAMOM AND RHUBARB CAKE

 Makes an 8-inch (20-cm) round cake

Have you started baking with cardamom yet? If not, you're definitely missing out. This is another fantastic cake that shows off the soft, collapsing flesh of beautiful rhubarb stems and the sweet, unmistakable flavor of cardamom that adds depth and warmth to it. The key is to not use too much. Cardamom should never be overpowering.

Macerated Rhubarb

10 oz (285 g) rhubarb, sliced thickly

¼ cup (50 g) granulated sugar

1 tsp vanilla extract

Cardamom and Rhubarb Cake

Canola oil spray, for pan

½ cup (114 g) unsalted butter, at room temperature, chopped roughly

1 cup (200 g) granulated sugar

3 large eggs

1½ cups (188 g) self-rising flour

1 tsp ground cardamom

¾ cup (180 ml) Greek yogurt

Powdered sugar, for dusting

Make the macerated rhubarb: Place the rhubarb in a bowl and sprinkle with the granulated sugar. Add the vanilla. Give it a good stir so all the rhubarb is covered, then set aside for 30 minutes to draw out some of the juices.

Make the cardamom and rhubarb cake: Preheat the oven to 350°F (177°C). Spray the base and sides of an 8-inch (20-cm) round, 3-inch (7.5-cm)-deep cake pan with canola oil and line the base with parchment paper.

In a large bowl, beat together the butter and granulated sugar until pale and fluffy. Add the eggs, one at a time, beating well after each addition. Gently, fold in the flour, cardamom and yogurt until well combined. Fold in half of the macerated rhubarb, about 6.5 ounces (185 g).

Pour the batter into the prepared pan. Dot the remaining rhubarb over the top of the batter. Bake for 65 to 75 minutes, or until a skewer inserted into the middle of the cake comes out clean. Remove the cake from the oven. Set it aside for 5 minutes, then carefully turn it out onto a wire rack.

Enjoy warm or at room temperature with a dusting of powdered sugar.

CHERRY CRUNCH CHEESECAKE

≫ Makes an 8-inch (20-cm) round cake ≪

This delicious cherry cheesecake combines the best of both worlds: a luscious cheesecake and a crunchy streusel top. You could call it a celebration of cherries because of the presence of luscious cherries in both layers. It's the perfect way to end a leisurely meal.

Cookie Crust

Canola oil spray, for pan

5 oz (150 g) graham crackers or digestive biscuits

⅓ cup (76 g) unsalted butter, melted

Cheesecake Filling

16 oz (455 g) cream cheese, at room temperature

½ cup (120 ml) sour cream

1 cup (200 g) granulated sugar

3 large eggs

1 tsp vanilla extract

⅓ cup (51 g) cherries, pitted

Crunch Topping

½ cup (45 g) rolled oats

¼ cup (31 g) all-purpose flour

¼ cup (55 g) light or dark brown sugar

3 tbsp (43 g) unsalted butter, chilled, chopped

½ cup (77 g) cherries, pitted

Make the cookie crust: Spray the base and sides of an 8-inch (20-cm) round, 3-inch (7.5-cm)-deep springform pan with canola oil and line the base with parchment paper. Place the springform pan on a baking sheet.

In a food processor, process the graham crackers until they resemble fine crumbs. Add the butter and process briefly until combined. Press the mixture evenly over the base of the prepared pan. Chill in the fridge for 30 minutes.

Make the cheesecake filling: In a large bowl, beat together the cream cheese, sour cream and granulated sugar until smooth and creamy. Add the eggs, one at a time, beating well after each addition. Add the vanilla and beat for 30 seconds. Fold in the cherries. Pour the filling over the cookie crust.

Make the crunch topping: Preheat the oven to 320°F (160°C). In a medium-sized bowl, stir together the oats, flour and brown sugar. Using your fingers, rub the butter into the mixture until it resembles coarse crumbs.

Assemble: Scatter the oat crumble over the cheesecake filling. Scatter the cherries on top of the crumble. Bake for 60 to 70 minutes, or until the crumble topping turns golden brown and the cheesecake filling is just set. It should still have a slight wobble to it.

Let the cheesecake cool in the oven with the oven door left slightly ajar. Refrigerate for at least 4 hours before serving.

PLUM AND GINGER CRUMBLE CAKE

≫ Makes an 8-inch (20-cm) round cake ≪

Why save ginger cakes just for the holidays? Even though this no-fuss cake doesn't need icing, it nonetheless packs a lot of flavor into each mouthful. When serving, dollop some whipped cream on top of each slice. You are welcome to add crystallized ginger to the batter for an extra ginger kick. The sweetest summer plums are used here; however, pears might work well in place of plums if they are not in season.

Plum and Ginger Cake

Canola oil spray, for pan

1⅓ cups (166 g) self-rising flour

⅓ cup (41 g) all-purpose flour

1 tsp ground ginger

⅔ cup (152 g) unsalted butter, at room temperature

¾ cup (150 g) granulated sugar

2 large eggs

½ cup (120 ml) milk

Crumble Topping

½ cup (63 g) all-purpose flour

¼ cup (55 g) firmly packed light or dark brown sugar

¼ cup (57 g) unsalted butter, chilled and cubed

2 tbsp (21 g) crystallized ginger, chopped finely

4 (296 g) plums, pitted, quartered

Make the plum and ginger cake: Preheat the oven to 350°F (177°C). Spray the base and sides of an 8-inch (20-cm) round, 3-inch (7.5-cm)-deep cake pan with canola oil and line the base with parchment paper.

Into a medium-sized bowl, sift the self-rising flour, all-purpose flour and ginger, and stir together.

In a large bowl, beat together the butter and granulated sugar until pale and fluffy. Add the eggs, one at a time, beating well after each addition. Fold in the flour mixture, alternating with the milk, until just combined. Transfer the batter to the prepared cake pan.

Make the crumble topping: In a small bowl, stir together the flour and brown sugar. Using your fingertips, rub the butter into the flour mixture until it resembles coarse bread crumbs. Add the crystallized ginger and stir to combine.

Assemble: Arrange the plums over the cake batter in the prepared pan. Sprinkle the crumble evenly over the plums. Bake for 60 to 65 minutes, or until a skewer inserted into the middle of the cake comes out clean. Remove the cake from the oven. Set it aside for 10 minutes, then gently run a blunt knife around the edges to loosen the cake. Carefully turn it out onto a wire rack to cool completely.

The cake is best enjoyed warm or at room temperature with a side of vanilla ice cream or whipped cream.

PASSION FRUIT LOAF

Passion fruit is unmatched in its ability to give desserts zing and flair. Throw cream cheese frosting into the mix and you have a loaf that becomes much more than simply a teatime treat. Great tea pairings with this passion fruit loaf would be Earl Grey, due to the presence of citrus in both the tea and the cake, or a tea with a delicate, floral profile, such as jasmine tea.

Passion Fruit Loaf

Canola oil spray, for pan

1 cup (227 g) unsalted butter, at room temperature

1 cup (200 g) granulated sugar

3 large eggs, at room temperature

1 tbsp (6 g) finely grated lemon zest

½ cup (120 ml) passion fruit puree

2 cups (250 g) self-rising flour

½ cup (120 ml) sour cream

Cream Cheese Frosting

4 oz (115 g) cream cheese (not low-fat), at room temperature

¼ cup (57 g) unsalted butter, at room temperature

1¼ cups (150 g) powdered sugar

1 tsp vanilla extract

For Assembly

¼ cup (60 ml) passion fruit puree, for drizzling

Make the passion fruit loaf: Preheat the oven to 350°F (177°C). Spray the base and sides of an 8 × 4–inch (20 × 10–cm), 3-inch (7.5-cm)-deep loaf pan with canola oil and line the base with parchment paper.

In a large bowl, beat together the butter and granulated sugar until pale and fluffy. Add the eggs, one at a time, beating well after each addition. Beat in the lemon zest and passion fruit puree. Alternately fold in the flour and sour cream, and stir until just combined.

Transfer the mixture to the prepared pan. Bake for 65 to 75 minutes, or until a skewer inserted into the middle of the loaf comes out clean. Remove the loaf from the oven. Set it aside for 5 minutes, then carefully turn it out onto a wire rack to cool completely.

Make the cream cheese frosting: In a medium-sized bowl, beat together the cream cheese and butter until smooth, about 2 minutes. Using a rubber spatula, scrape down the sides of the bowl to ensure that the mixture is evenly mixed. Beat in the powdered sugar, a little at a time, until well incorporated. Add the vanilla. Mix until combined.

Assemble: Once the loaf has cooled to room temperature, dollop with the cream cheese frosting, or pipe it on using a piping bag fitted with a round nozzle. Drizzle the passion fruit puree over the cream cheese frosting.

THE FUDGIEST BROWNIE CAKE

Moist, fudgy, nutty and outrageously decadent, thanks to the secret ingredient—cream cheese. The addition of dried figs is optional but highly recommended. Top with fresh raspberries and serve with vanilla ice cream, and you have a dessert that will draw gasps from even the non–sweet lovers.

Canola oil spray, for pan

¾ cup (170 g) unsalted butter

3 oz (85 g) dark chocolate, chopped roughly

⅓ cup (35 g) Dutch-processed cocoa powder, plus more for serving

1¼ cups (250 g) sugar

1 tsp vanilla extract

3 large eggs, at room temperature

3 oz (85 g) cream cheese, at room temperature, diced

½ cup (63 g) all-purpose flour

½ cup (55 g) pecans or walnuts, chopped and toasted

¼ cup (25 g) dried figs, sliced (optional)

Fresh raspberries, for serving (optional)

Preheat the oven to 350°F (177°C). Spray the base and sides of an 8-inch (20-cm) round, 3-inch (7.5-cm)-deep cake pan with canola oil and line the base with parchment paper.

In a large saucepan, combine the butter and chocolate, and melt over low heat, stirring frequently. Remove the pan from the heat. Beat in the cocoa powder, sugar and vanilla. Add the eggs, one at a time, beating well after each addition. Beat in the cream cheese, then fold in the flour, nuts and figs (if using).

Pour the batter into the prepared pan. Smooth the top with the back of a spoon or an offset spatula. Bake for 45 to 50 minutes, or until a skewer inserted into the middle of the cake comes out with a few moist crumbs. Take care not to overbake the cake, as the secret to a fudgy brownie is slightly undercooking it.

Remove the cake from the oven. Allow to cool for 15 minutes in the pan, then turn it out onto a wire rack to cool completely. Slice and serve warm or at room temperature with fresh raspberries (if using) or a dusting of cocoa powder.

IRRESISTIBLE FUNFETTI CAKE

Makes a 9-inch (23-cm) round cake

Every year for my cousin's birthday, my Aunt Ilapi made the most delicious cake. Although it was only a plain chocolate cake with Cadbury Gems decorations, the happiness it brought was immeasurable. It was every child's dream! This cake is a tribute to my aunt, who has preserved the magic and delight of cakes to this day. This recipe produces the ideal homemade birthday cake and swaps out the Gem candies for rainbow sprinkles.

Funfetti Cake

Canola oil spray, for pan

¾ cup (170 g) unsalted butter, at room temperature

1 cup + 2 tbsp (226 g) granulated sugar

2 large eggs, at room temperature

2 tsp (10 ml) vanilla extract

1½ cups (188 g) all-purpose flour

1 tsp baking powder

2 tbsp (16 g) cornstarch

¾ cup (180 ml) milk

1 cup (203 g) rainbow sprinkles, divided

Vanilla Buttercream

1 cup (227 g) unsalted butter, at room temperature

4 cups (480 g) powdered sugar

1 tbsp (15 ml) vanilla extract

3 tbsp (45 ml) whole milk

Make the funfetti cake: Preheat the oven to 350°F (177°C). Spray the base and sides of a 9-inch (23-cm) round, 3-inch (7.5-cm)-deep cake pan with canola oil and line the base with parchment paper.

In a large bowl, beat together the butter and granulated sugar until pale and fluffy. Add the eggs, one at a time, beating well after each addition. Beat in the vanilla.

In a separate bowl, mix together the flour, baking powder and cornstarch. In alternate batches, add the flour mixture and milk to the butter mixture while beating on low speed, until just combined. Fold in ½ cup (102 g) of the sprinkles.

Transfer the batter to the prepared pan and smooth out the surface with a spatula.

Bake for 60 to 75 minutes, or until a skewer inserted into the middle of the cake comes out clean. Remove the pan from the oven. Set it aside for 10 minutes, then gently run a blunt knife around the edges to loosen the cake. Carefully turn it out onto a wire rack to cool completely.

Make the vanilla buttercream: In a large bowl, using an electric mixer, beat the butter until light and fluffy, 4 to 5 minutes. Add the powdered sugar, a little at a time, beating constantly until well combined. Scrape down the sides of the bowl as and when required. Add the vanilla and milk, and beat until smooth.

Assemble: Place the cooled cake on a serving plate or cake stand. Using a piping bag fitted with a closed star tip, pipe swirls of buttercream on the top of the cake in two circles, leaving a small space in the middle for the sprinkles. Decorate the center and the swirls with the remaining ½ cup (102 g) sprinkles.

EARL GREY CAKE WITH STRAWBERRY ICING

Makes a 7-inch (18-cm) round cake

Sprinkle a little wow factor over your next tea party by serving this light cake with citrus notes. You'll want to bake with the Earl Grey flavor frequently after you've tasted it. The irresistible appeal of bergamot oranges from the tea and strawberries when combined is what makes the cake so alluring. Fresh strawberries give the mouthwateringly delectable strawberry icing its natural pink color.

Earl Grey Cake
Canola oil spray, for pan

1 Earl Grey tea bag

¼ cup (60 ml) boiling water

½ cup (114 g) unsalted butter, at room temperature

⅔ cup (133 g) granulated sugar

2 large eggs

1 tbsp (15 ml) milk

1¼ cups (156 g) self-rising flour

Strawberry Icing
⅓ cup (55 g) strawberries, washed, hulled and sliced

1½ cups (180 g) powdered sugar

For Assembly
Edible flowers

Make the Earl Grey cake: Preheat the oven to 350°F (177°C). Spray the base and sides of a 7-inch (18-cm) round, 3-inch (7.5-cm)-deep cake pan with canola oil and line the base with parchment paper.

Empty the tea leaves from the tea bag into a cup and add the boiling water. Set aside for 10 minutes to infuse. Strain the tea, discarding the leaves, and allow to cool to room temperature.

In a large bowl, beat together the butter and granulated sugar until pale and fluffy. Add the eggs, one at a time, beating well after each addition. Add the brewed tea, milk and flour, and beat until pale and creamy.

Transfer the mixture to the prepared pan. Bake for 55 to 65 minutes, or until a skewer inserted into the middle of the cake comes out clean. Remove the cake from the oven. Set it aside for 15 minutes, then carefully loosen the edges with a blunt knife. The cake is soft and moist, so care needs to be taken while turning it out onto a wire rack. Allow to cool completely before icing the cake.

Make the strawberry icing: In a blender or food processor, puree the strawberries. Measure out 2 tablespoons (30 ml) of the puree. Add the powdered sugar and mix until smooth. If the icing is too thick, add more puree, ½ teaspoon at a time. If it is too thin, add in more powdered sugar until the desired consistency is reached.

Assemble: Once the cake has cooled, drizzle with the icing, allowing some of it to fall down the sides. Set the cake aside for 15 to 20 minutes for the icing to set. Once the icing has become firm, decorate with edible flowers.

STONE FRUIT CAKE

⇒ Makes a 9-inch (23-cm) round cake ⇐

We produced a lot of reports back in the hectic corporate days when I used to work for a bank. Large spreadsheets of information, or MISs as they were known, had to be shared with teams and managers. My exuberant and enterprising supervisor made it apparent that the headers needed to be accentuated in bright colors to break up the monotony. "Use a lot of orange and red," he would advise, "and avoid using gray because it is a dreary color." I still follow his advice. Thankfully, nature gives us enough oranges and reds to choose from in the form of gorgeous fresh fruits. For this lovely summer cake, utilize all the colorful fruits you can find. You could use Candied Herbs (page 152) to increase the oomph factor.

Stone Fruit Cake

Canola oil spray, for pan

1⅔ cups (208 g) self-rising flour

½ cup (51 g) almond meal

1 tsp ground cinnamon

½ cup (114 g) unsalted butter, at room temperature

1 cup (220 g) light or dark brown sugar

3 large eggs

1 tsp vanilla extract

1 cup (240 ml) Greek yogurt

1 yellow nectarine, pitted, chopped

1 yellow peach, pitted, chopped

1 plum, pitted, chopped

1 apricot, pitted, chopped

5-6 cherries, pitted, chopped

Ricotta Frosting

¼ cup (58 g) cream cheese, at room temperature

½ cup (123 g) firm ricotta cheese, at room temperature

¼ cup (60 ml) heavy cream

1 cup (120 g) powdered sugar

½ tsp ground cardamom, or 1 tsp vanilla extract

For Assembly

1 yellow nectarine, pitted, sliced thinly

1 yellow peach, pitted, sliced thinly

1 plum, pitted, sliced thinly

1 apricot, pitted, quartered

7 to 8 cherries

Make the stone fruit cake: Preheat the oven to 350°F (177°C). Spray the base and sides of a 9-inch (23-cm) round, 3-inch (7.5-cm)-deep cake pan with canola oil and line the base with parchment paper.

In a medium-sized bowl, stir together the flour, almond meal and cinnamon.

In a large bowl, beat together the butter and brown sugar until pale and fluffy. Add the eggs, one at a time, beating well after each addition. Beat in the vanilla.

Fold in the flour mixture, alternating with the yogurt, until just combined. Fold in the chopped nectarine, peach, plum, apricot and cherries.

Transfer the batter to the prepared cake pan. Bake for 60 to 65 minutes, or until a skewer inserted into the middle of the cake comes out clean. Remove the cake from the oven. Set it aside for 10 minutes, then gently run a blunt knife around the edges to loosen the cake. Carefully turn it out onto a wire rack to cool completely.

Make the ricotta frosting: Using an electric mixer, beat the cream cheese until pale and fluffy, about 2 minutes. Add the ricotta, cream, powdered sugar and cardamom, then beat on high speed until the mixture starts to look thick and holds soft peaks, 4 to 5 minutes.

Assemble: Dollop the ricotta frosting onto the cooled cake. Decorate the top with the sliced nectarine, peach and plum, plus the quartered apricot. Top with the cherries.

BANANA CAKE WITH BLACK SESAME SWIRLS

You'll have to excuse anybody who inquires about the source of this lovely banana bread. The marbling effect, which not only looks incredible but tastes even better, is made possible by the addition of tahini and black sesame seeds. It requires just one batter, keeping things simple and achievable for even the novice baker.

Canola oil spray, for pan

½ cup (114 g) unsalted butter, at room temperature

½ cup (100 g) sugar

2 large eggs

2 large ripe bananas (about 9 oz [250 g]), mashed

1 tsp vanilla extract

1½ cups (188 g) self-rising flour

1 tsp baking soda

¼ cup (60 ml) milk

2 tbsp (30 g) tahini

2 tbsp (30 g) black sesame powder (see Note)

Preheat the oven to 350°F (177°C). Spray the base and sides of an 8 × 4–inch (20 × 10–cm), 3-inch (7.5-cm)-deep loaf pan with canola oil and line the base with parchment paper.

In a large bowl, beat together the butter and sugar until pale and fluffy. Add the eggs, one at a time, beating well after each addition. Add the bananas, vanilla extract, flour, baking soda and milk. Beat until just combined.

Transfer half of the batter to another bowl and mix in the tahini and black sesame powder.

Drop alternating scoops of the banana batter and the black sesame batter into the prepared pan. Using a bamboo skewer, make swirls in the batter.

Bake for 50 to 60 minutes, or until a skewer inserted into the middle of the loaf comes out clean. Remove the loaf from the oven. Set it aside for 5 minutes, then carefully turn it out onto a wire rack to cool completely.

NOTE: Black sesame powder is available in Asian stores and some supermarkets. If you are unable to source it, make your own by pulsing the seeds in a spice grinder (or using a mortar and pestle) until they are still powdery, just shy of releasing their natural oils. The finished loaf cake doesn't care whether the black sesame powder is gritty or slightly wet, so don't worry too much about it.

ORANGE OLIVE OIL CAKE

⇒ Makes an 8-inch (20-cm) round cake ⇐

This is my blueprint recipe for all citrus-based olive oil cakes. I've made it with blood oranges, lemons and limes. It's the simplest of cakes, yet it's light, refreshing and always delicious. You may keep it as basic or glam as you wish by adding dehydrated orange slices (page 155).

Canola oil spray, for pan

3 large eggs

1 cup (200 g) granulated sugar

¾ cup (180 ml) extra virgin olive oil

¼ cup (60 ml) fresh orange juice

1 cup (125 g) self-rising flour

½ cup (51 g) almond meal

1 tbsp (6 g) finely grated orange zest

3 tbsp (60 g) orange marmalade

Powdered sugar, for dusting (optional)

Sliced oranges, for garnish

Preheat the oven to 350°F (177°C). Spray the base and sides of an 8-inch (20-cm) round, 3-inch (7.5-cm)-deep cake pan with canola oil and line the base with parchment paper.

In a large bowl, using an electric mixer, beat together the eggs and granulated sugar until thick and pale, 4 to 5 minutes. Add the olive oil and juice, and beat until just combined.

Add the flour, almond meal and orange zest, and use a metal spoon to gently fold in until combined. Do not overmix the batter.

Transfer the batter to the prepared pan. Bake for 55 to 60 minutes, or until a skewer inserted into the middle of the cake comes out clean. Remove the pan from the oven. Set it aside for 10 minutes, then gently run a blunt knife around the edges to loosen the cake. Carefully turn it out onto a wire rack to cool completely.

Assemble: In a microwave-safe bowl, warm the marmalade for 10 seconds in a microwave, then spread it over the top of the cooled cake. Dust with powdered sugar, if desired. Decorate with sliced oranges.

LEMON RASPBERRY LOAF

Lemon and raspberries complement each other so well. This zingy, invigorating loaf is the perfect accompaniment to a cup of tea. For a nuttier version, add 2 tablespoons (17 g) of poppy seeds to the batter. If you're making it for a special occasion, add a few slices of Dehydrated Citrus (page 155) for visual appeal.

Lemon Raspberry Loaf

Canola oil spray, for pan

½ cup (114 g) unsalted butter, at room temperature

¾ cup (150 g) granulated sugar

2 large eggs

1 tbsp (6 g) lemon zest

¼ cup (60 ml) fresh lemon juice

1½ cups (188 g) self-rising flour

¼ cup (60 ml) milk

1 cup (123 g) raspberries (fresh or frozen)

Yogurt Glaze

2 tbsp (30 ml) Greek yogurt

1 tsp lemon zest

1¼ cups (150 g) powdered sugar

For Assembly

Fresh raspberries, for garnish

Make the lemon raspberry loaf: Preheat the oven to 350°F (177°C). Spray the base and sides of an 8 × 4–inch (20 × 10–cm), 3-inch (7.5-cm)-deep loaf pan with canola oil and line the base with parchment paper.

In a large bowl, beat together the butter and granulated sugar until pale and fluffy. Add the eggs, one at a time, beating well after each addition. Add the lemon zest and juice. Beat until just combined.

Fold in the flour, alternating with the milk, until the mixture is just combined. Fold in the raspberries. Bake for 45 to 50 minutes, or until a skewer inserted into the middle of the loaf comes out clean. Remove the loaf from the oven. Set it aside for 5 minutes, then carefully turn it out onto a wire rack to cool completely.

Make the yogurt glaze: In a medium-sized bowl, beat together the yogurt, lemon zest and powdered sugar until smooth.

Assemble: Place the loaf on a serving tray or plate. Drizzle the loaf with yogurt glaze. Top with fresh raspberries.

EFFORTLESS SHOWSTOPPERS

What's the one the one thing that is always in style? An eye-popping showstopper cake that is also ridiculously easy to make. It makes you look savvy and like someone who knows their game. Who said impressive has to be elaborate?

This chapter is about having fun while unleashing the creative baker in you.

A unique garnish, an eye-catching pattern in the batter, some unexpected yet amazing flavor pairings or a unique spin on a classic turn these ordinary cakes into a spectacular culinary centerpiece. These showstopping desserts won't take all day to make, but they will guarantee that your dinner guests talk about them for days.

Take your red velvet cake game to the next level by adding a double dose of raspberries. It's not just a tasty surprise, but a game changer. I had so much fun playing with the batter and filling of the Mango Cake with Basil Cream Cheese Swirl (page 70) and the Blueberry Zebra Cheesecake (page 81). Watch people gasp as you slice into these beauties. Wake up your inner child with the Apple, Pear and Blueberry Cake with marzipan fruits (page 69). If you've loved Play-Doh® as a child, here's your chance of doing it as an adult. And eating it, too!

Who are the real showstoppers? They are the people who create magic in their kitchen. The people behind the bakes who put a lot of love into the food, so much so that the person tasting it can feel that powerful magic and sense that love. People like you. More often than not, we express ourselves through food. It's a spiritual connection. I hope these cakes help you make that connection with the people you cherish.

APPLE, PEAR AND BLUEBERRY CAKE

≫ Makes a 7-inch (18-cm) round cake ≪

A perfect symphony of apples, pears, blueberries and cinnamon creates a soft, moist cake full of texture. You can keep it simple as you like by skipping the marzipan fruits, or turn it into a showstopper for your next gathering. The cake is a blank canvas for you to decorate the marzipan fruits according to the occasion. Pink and fuchsia for Valentine's day. Black and gray for Halloween. The possibilities are endless!

Apple, Pear and Blueberry Cake
Canola oil spray, for pan

1 cup (125 g) all-purpose flour

1 tsp baking powder

1 tsp ground cinnamon

½ cup (114 g) unsalted butter, softened

½ cup (100 g) granulated sugar

2 large eggs

¼ cup (60 ml) milk

2 medium-sized apples, cored, peeled and chopped into ¾" (2-cm) cubes

2 pears, cored, peeled and chopped into ¾" (2-cm) cubes

½ cup (74 g) blueberries

Cinnamon Sour Cream Glaze
½ cup (120 ml) sour cream, cold

1 cup (120 g) powdered sugar

½ tsp ground cinnamon

For Assembly
Blueberries

Marzipan Fruits (page 151, optional)

Meringue Kisses (page 156)

Edible flowers

Make the apple, pear and blueberry cake: Preheat the oven to 350°F (177°C). Spray the base and sides of a 7-inch (18-cm) round, 3-inch (7.5-cm)-deep cake pan with canola oil and line the base with parchment paper.

Into a medium-sized bowl, sift the flour, baking powder and cinnamon.

In a separate large bowl, beat together the butter and granulated sugar until light and fluffy. Add the eggs, one at a time, beating well after each addition.

Alternately fold the flour and milk into the butter mixture. Then, fold in the cubed apples and pears and the blueberries.

Pour the batter into the prepared pan. Bake for 1 hour 10 minutes, or until a skewer inserted into the middle of the cake comes out clean. Remove the cake from the oven and allow to cool for 10 minutes. Then, turn it out onto a wire rack to cool completely before glazing.

While the cake cools, make the cinnamon sour cream glaze: In a small bowl, stir together the sour cream, powdered sugar and cinnamon until smooth.

Assemble: Pour the glaze on the cooled cake and allow to set, about 30 minutes. Decorate with blueberries, Marzipan Fruits (if using), Meringue Kisses and edible flowers.

MANGO CAKE WITH BASIL CREAM CHEESE SWIRL

≫ Makes an 8-inch (20-cm) round cake ≪

Part cheesecake, part cake, 100 percent divine! Basil and mango have separate flavor qualities, yet they miraculously meld together in this swirling showstopper. Like the Netflix mother and daughter duo Ginny and Georgia—cute, unique, but quite the force when combined. Use candied basil (page 152) to garnish if you're a fan of the herb.

Mango Cake

Canola oil spray, for pan

½ cup (114 g) unsalted butter, at room temperature

½ cup (100 g) sugar

2 large eggs

1 cup (125 g) self-rising flour

¼ tsp baking soda

1 cup (240 ml) mango puree

Mango Sauce

½ cup (120 ml) mango puree

1 tbsp (13 g) sugar

1 tsp cornstarch

Basil Cream Cheese Layer

8 oz (226 g) cream cheese, room temperature

½ cup (100 g) sugar

1 large egg

¼ cup (31 g) all-purpose flour

3 tbsp (8 g) fresh whole basil leaves

2 or 3 drops green food coloring (optional)

For Assembly

Fresh mango cubes

Fresh basil leaves or candied basil (page 152)

Make the mango cake: Preheat the oven to 350°F (177°C). Spray the base and sides of an 8-inch (20-cm) round, 3-inch (7.5-cm)-deep cake pan with canola oil and line the base with parchment paper.

In a large bowl, beat together the butter and sugar until pale and fluffy. Add the eggs, one at a time, beating well after each addition.

Fold in the flour and baking soda, alternating with the mango puree. Mix until just combined.

Make the mango sauce: In a small saucepan, combine the mango puree, sugar and cornstarch. Whisk well to ensure there are no lumps. Cook the mixture over low heat, stirring constantly until it thickens to form a sauce. Remove the pan from the heat. Allow the sauce to cool to room temperature. The sauce can be stored in the fridge until needed.

Make the basil cream cheese layer: In a blender, combine the cream cheese, sugar, egg, flour and basil. Blend until the mixture is smooth. It should turn light green. Add the food coloring (if using) and blend until uniform.

Assemble: Spread a thick layer of the mango cake batter in the prepared pan, extending it outward toward the edges by tilting the pan. Add a scoop of basil cream cheese batter on top of the batter. Continue to add a scoop of each batter, alternating with each other, until all the batter is used up, wiggling the pan gently to level out the batters.

Bake for 60 to 65 minutes, or until a skewer inserted into the middle of the cake comes out clean. Remove the cake from the oven. Set it aside for 10 minutes, then gently run a blunt knife around the edges to loosen the cake. Carefully turn it out onto a wire rack to cool completely.

Once the cake has cooled, spread the mango sauce over the top, allowing some to drip over the edges. Top with fresh mango cubes and fresh or candied basil leaves. Slice and serve.

RED VELVET CAKE WITH RASPBERRIES

≫ Makes a 7-inch (18-cm) round cake ≪

When I first had a red velvet cake as a fully grown adult, I immediately regretted all the years of my life that I had squandered not knowing it existed. Of course, I'm being dramatic, but this cake is so good that a little drama is appropriate.

Please do not leave out the raspberry coulis. It's a double whammy of sweet raspberry flavor in one seriously amazing cake. The cake becomes a holiday showstopper when decorated with Meringue Kisses (page 156) over the frosting.

Red Velvet Cake

Canola oil spray, for pan

⅓ cup + 1 tbsp (90 g) unsalted butter, at room temperature

¾ cup (150 g) granulated sugar

1 tsp vanilla extract

1 large egg

1¼ cups (156 g) self-rising flour

1 tbsp (5 g) Dutch-processed cocoa powder

½ cup (120 ml) buttermilk

1 tsp distilled white vinegar

1 tsp baking soda

½ tsp red gel food coloring or 1 tsp liquid food coloring

Raspberry Coulis

1 cup (123 g) fresh raspberries

2 tbsp (26 g) granulated sugar

2 tbsp (30 ml) water

Cream Cheese Frosting

4 oz (115 g) cream cheese (not low-fat), at room temperature

¼ cup (57 g) unsalted butter, at room temperature

1¼ cups (150 g) powdered sugar

1 tsp vanilla extract

For Assembly

1 pint (246 g) fresh raspberries

Make the red velvet cake: Preheat the oven to 350°F (177°C). Spray the base and sides of a 7-inch (18-cm) round, 3-inch (7.5-cm)-deep cake pan with canola oil and line the base with parchment paper.

In a large bowl, beat together the butter, granulated sugar and vanilla until pale and fluffy. Add the egg and beat well.

Add the flour, cocoa powder and buttermilk in batches, and beat until well combined. Finally, add the vinegar, baking soda and food coloring, and stir to combine.

Transfer the mixture to the prepared pan. Bake for 45 to 50 minutes, or until a skewer inserted into the middle of the cake comes out clean. Remove the pan from the oven. Set it aside for 10 minutes, then gently run a blunt knife around the edges to loosen the cake. Carefully turn it out onto a wire rack to cool completely.

Make the raspberry coulis: In a small saucepan, combine the raspberries, granulated sugar and water, and simmer over low heat until the sugar has melted and the mixture has thickened slightly.

Transfer the mixture to a blender and puree until smooth. Strain the coulis into a small bowl. Store in the refrigerator until needed.

Make the cream cheese frosting: In a medium-sized bowl, beat together the cream cheese and butter until smooth, about 2 minutes. Using a rubber spatula, scrape down the sides of the bowl to ensure that the mixture is evenly mixed. Beat in the powdered sugar, a little at a time, until well incorporated. Add the vanilla and mix until incorporated.

Assemble: Once the cake has cooled to room temperature, pipe the cream cheese frosting, using a piping bag fitted with a round nozzle, over the top of the cake. Using a pastry brush, brush the raspberry coulis over the frosting. Arrange the fresh raspberries in between the piped mounds of frosting. Using a piping bag or a small spoon, fill up the hollow in each raspberry with raspberry coulis. The cake is best enjoyed at room temperature or slightly cold.

HAZELNUT AND COFFEE CAKE

➢ Makes a 7-inch (18-cm) round cake ➢

The combination of coffee and hazelnuts is unbeatable. Candied hazelnuts are the crowning glory on this coffee-spiked cake that is glazed with a thick layer of ganache. It's outrageously delicious and equally easy to make. I dare you not to devour the cooled candied hazelnuts right off the pan.

Hazelnut and Coffee Cake

Canola oil spray, for pan

1 tbsp (9 g) instant coffee powder

½ cup (120 ml) milk

½ cup (114 g) unsalted butter

1 cup (220 g) light or dark brown sugar

2 medium-sized eggs

1 cup (125 g) self-rising flour

½ cup (102 g) hazelnut meal

Chocolate Ganache

½ cup (120 ml) heavy cream

4 oz (120 g) dark chocolate, chopped into small pieces

For Assembly

Caramel Shards, candied hazelnuts variation (page 159)

Make the hazelnut and coffee cake: Preheat the oven to 350°F (177°C). Spray the base and sides of a 7-inch (18-cm) round, 3-inch (7.5-cm)-deep cake pan with canola oil and line the base with parchment paper.

In a small bowl, combine the coffee powder and milk. Stir until the coffee is dissolved. Set aside until needed.

In a large bowl, beat together the butter and brown sugar until pale and fluffy. Add the eggs, one at a time, beating well after each addition.

Fold in the flour, hazelnut meal and milk mixture, in alternating batches, until combined. Transfer the batter to the prepared pan and smooth out the surface with a spatula.

Bake for 55 to 65 minutes, or until a skewer inserted into the middle of the cake comes out clean. Remove the pan from the oven. Set it aside for 10 minutes, then gently run a blunt knife around the edges to loosen the cake. Carefully turn it out onto a wire rack to cool completely.

Make the chocolate ganache: In a medium-sized microwave-safe bowl, combine the cream and chocolate. Microwave on medium (50%) for 2 to 3 minutes, removing the bowl and stirring every 30 seconds with a metal spoon until smooth. Set aside for 5 minutes to cool down slightly.

Assemble: Place the cooled cake on a cake plate or stand. Spread the chocolate ganache on top. Decorate with the candied hazelnuts.

WHITE FOREST CAKE

I've taken everything you love about a traditional Black Forest cake and upped the ante by making it with white chocolate. Desiccated coconut gives the cake its distinct coconut flavor, while shredded coconut gives it a dreamy, wintery appearance. This one really is the cherry on top!

White Forest Cake

Canola oil spray, for pan

¾ cup (170 g) unsalted butter, at room temperature

1 cup (200 g) granulated sugar

3 large eggs

1½ cups (188 g) self-rising flour

½ cup (47 g) desiccated coconut

¾ cup (180 ml) Greek yogurt

16 oz (455 g) pitted black or sour cherries in syrup, drained, syrup reserved

½ cup (120 ml) cherry syrup from the can

Whipped Cream Frosting

1 cup (240 ml) heavy cream or thickened cream, cold

2 tbsp (16 g) powdered sugar

1 tsp vanilla extract

For Assembly

1 cup (100 g) sweetened shredded coconut

3.5 oz (100 g) white chocolate, grated

8 to 10 fresh cherries, for garnish

Make the white forest cake: Preheat the oven to 350°F (177°C). Spray the base and sides of an 8-inch (20-cm) round, 3-inch (7.5-cm)-deep cake pan with canola oil and line the base with parchment paper.

In a large bowl, beat together the butter and granulated sugar until pale and fluffy. Add the eggs, one at a time, beating well after each addition.

Fold in the flour, alternating with the desiccated coconut and yogurt. Fold in the drained cherries.

Transfer the batter to the prepared cake pan. Bake for 60 to 65 minutes, or until a skewer inserted into the middle of the cake comes out clean. Remove the cake from the oven. Set it aside for 10 minutes, then gently run a blunt knife around the edges to loosen the cake. Carefully turn it out onto a wire rack. While the cake is still warm, poke holes with a skewer all over the surface of the cake. Drizzle the reserved cherry syrup over the holes. Allow the cake to cool down to room temperature.

Make the whipped cream frosting: With an electric mixer, whisk the cream on medium speed until frothy. Add the powdered sugar and vanilla, and continue to beat until stiff peaks form, 4 to 5 minutes. Store in the refrigerator until needed.

Assemble: Place the cooled cake on a cake stand or plate. On a shallow plate, mix together the shredded coconut and grated white chocolate. Using an offset spatula, cover the top and sides of the cake with whipped cream frosting. Transfer the remaining frosting to a piping bag fitted with an open star tip. Pipe swirls onto the top of the cake. Sprinkle the sides of the cake with white chocolate mixture, pressing gently with the palm of your hand to adhere. Decorate with the fresh cherries. Since it has been frosted with whipped cream, this cake is best kept refrigerated and consumed within 1 day.

CARAMEL POACHED PEAR AND SPICED WHITE CHOCOLATE CAKE

⇒ Makes a 7-inch (18-cm) round cake ⇐

Although white chocolate is the star of this recipe, the addition of the spices guarantees that the sweetness is not overpowering and that there is a balance of the sweet and spicy flavors. Caramel poached pears are the ideal accompaniment to a spice-infused dessert. The mere sight of the smooth, glistening flesh drenched in golden caramel is enough to get the mouth salivating.

Caramel Poached Pears

3 cups (710 ml) water

½ cup (110 g) plus 1 tbsp (14 g) light or dark brown sugar, divided

3 to 4 whole star anise

2 sticks cinnamon

2 strips orange peel (about 1" [2.5 cm] wide each)

4 firm ripe pears (about 712 g) peeled, cored and halved

¼ cup (60 ml) heavy cream

2 tbsp (28 g) unsalted butter

Spiced White Chocolate Cake

Canola oil spray, for pan

1¼ cups (156 g) self-rising flour

1 tsp ground cinnamon

1 tsp ground cardamom

1 tsp ground nutmeg

⅔ cup (152 g) unsalted butter, at room temperature

¾ cup (150 g) granulated sugar

3 large eggs

¼ cup (60 ml) milk

3.5 oz (100 g) white chocolate, chopped finely

For Assembly

Dehydrated Citrus, for garnish (page 155)

Make the caramel poached pears: In a medium-sized saucepan, combine the water, ½ cup (110 g) of brown sugar, star anise, cinnamon and orange peel. Cook over medium heat until the mixture starts to boil. Lower the heat to low and add the pears. Bring to a gentle simmer, then cover the pan and continue to cook, turning the pears occasionally, until they are tender, about 1 hour.

Remove the pears from the syrup. Increase the heat to high and bring the syrup to a boil. Cook, uncovered, until the syrup thickens, about 10 minutes.

When you have about ¼ cup (60 ml) of syrup in the pan, lower the heat to low and add the cream, butter and remaining tablespoon (14 g) of the brown sugar. Cook until the sugar has dissolved and the mixture thickens slightly to form a caramel sauce. Remove the sauce from the heat and allow to cool. The caramel sauce will thicken further upon cooling.

Make the spiced white chocolate cake: Preheat the oven to 350°F (177°C). Spray the base and sides of a 7-inch (18-cm) round, 3-inch (7.5-cm)-deep cake pan with canola oil and line the base with parchment paper.

In a medium-sized bowl, stir together the flour, cinnamon, cardamom and nutmeg.

In a large bowl, beat together the butter and granulated sugar until pale and fluffy. Add the eggs, one at a time, beating well after each addition.

Fold the flour mixture, alternating with the milk, into the butter mixture, and mix until well combined. Fold in the white chocolate.

Transfer the batter to the prepared cake pan. Bake for 50 to 55 minutes, or until a skewer inserted into the middle of the cake comes out clean. Remove the cake from the oven. Set it aside for 10 minutes, then gently run a blunt knife around the edges to loosen the cake. Carefully turn it out onto a wire rack to cool completely.

Assemble: Place the cooled cake on a cake stand or serving plate. Top with the poached pears. Drizzle with the caramel sauce. Decorate with dehydrated citrus slices.

BLUEBERRY ZEBRA CHEESECAKE

꩜ Makes an 8-inch (20-cm) round cake ꩜

The zebra trend isn't reserved for the fashion conscious alone. Despite how intricate it might seem, the cheesecake is constructed of one batter. It's just a vanilla cheesecake that has been marbled with blueberry cheesecake batter. This one is sure to make a bold fashion statement at your upcoming gathering, but what makes it so enticing is the creamy deliciousness.

Blueberry Puree
1 cup (148 g) blueberries
2 tbsp (26 g) sugar
2 tbsp (30 ml) water

Cheesecake Crust
Canola oil spray, for pan
5 oz (150 g) graham crackers or digestive biscuits
⅓ cup (76 g) unsalted butter

Cheesecake Filling
½ cup (120 ml) milk
1 tbsp (9.4 g) powdered gelatin
11 oz (312 g) cream cheese, at room temperature
½ cup (100 g) sugar
1 cup (240 ml) heavy cream
1 tsp vanilla extract

1 cup (148 g) blueberries, for garnish

Make the blueberry puree: In a small saucepan, combine the blueberries, sugar and water over low heat. Bring to a boil, stirring constantly, until the blueberries soften and the mixture is thick. Using the back of a spoon, lightly crush the blueberries for a puree-like consistency. Strain the mixture.

Make the cheesecake crust: Spray the base and sides of an 8-inch (20-cm) round, 3-inch (7.5-cm)-deep springform pan with canola oil and line the base with parchment paper. Place the springform pan on a baking sheet.

In a food processor, process the graham crackers until they resemble fine crumbs. Add the butter and process briefly until combined. Press the mixture evenly over the base of the prepared pan. Place the pan in the fridge for 30 minutes to chill.

Make the cheesecake filling: In a small saucepan, place the milk and sprinkle the gelatin over it. Allow the gelatin to bloom for 5 minutes. Cook the milk over low heat, stirring constantly until the gelatin dissolves (do not boil the milk). Remove from the heat and allow to cool to room temperature.

In a large bowl, beat together the cream cheese and sugar until smooth and creamy. Add the cream and vanilla, and continue to beat until well blended and fluffy. Add the gelatin mixture and beat until just combined.

Divide the cheesecake filling equally between two bowls. I had about 14 ounces (400 g) of filling in each bowl. In one of the bowls, mix the blueberry puree into the filling.

Pour 6 tablespoons (90 ml) of the blueberry filling over the crust. Swirl the pan gently and allow the filling to flow outward. Drop 2 tablespoons (30 ml) of the plain (white) filling in the center directly above the blueberry filling. Pouring from a height will allow the filling to keep moving outward. Gently tap the pan in between if the filling does not flow automatically. Repeat with 2 tablespoons (30 ml) of the blueberry filling. Continue this process until all the filling is used up. The filling will start to look like concentric circles. Using a wooden skewer, create a pattern on top of the cheesecake.

Place the cheesecake in the fridge. Allow to set for 6 to 8 hours, preferable overnight. Once ready to serve, decorate with fresh blueberries.

BERRY CHARLOTTE

 Makes an 8-inch (20-cm) round cake

Although this cake requires some effort, it is a wonderful pleasure! This is the one you make for your best buddies. Cooking down a mixture of berries gives the berry *bavarois*, or berry mousse, its rich berry flavor that perfectly complements the circle of ladyfingers that enclose it. Sponge ladyfingers aren't simply for tiramisu. They play a vital role in constructing this magnificent, edible work of art. Allow fresh berries to adorn the top or get creative with Meringue Kisses (page 156).

Simple Syrup
½ cup (120 ml) water
1 tbsp (13 g) sugar

Berry Puree
2 cups (280 g) mixed berries
2 tbsp (30 ml) water
¼ cup (50 g) sugar
5 tsp (16 g) powdered gelatin

Berry Bavarois
6 large egg yolks
1 cup (200 g) sugar
2 tbsp (16 g) cornstarch
½ cup (120 ml) whole milk
1 tsp vanilla extract
1½ cups (360 ml) heavy cream, divided

Make the simple syrup: In a small saucepan, bring the water and sugar to a boil. Continue to cook until the sugar dissolves, about 5 minutes. Remove the saucepan from the heat and pour the syrup into a small cup or bowl. Set it aside to cool to room temperature.

Make the berry puree: In a small saucepan, combine the berries, water and sugar. Cook over low heat, stirring frequently, until the mixture reaches a simmer. Increase the heat to medium and continue to cook until the berries have broken down and the puree has thickened, about 15 minutes. Remove the pan from the heat and strain the puree, pressing on the fruit with the back of a spoon to extract as much puree as you can. You should have about ½ cup (120 ml) of puree.

Pour the puree back into the saucepan. Set it aside to cool for 15 minutes, then sprinkle the gelatin over the mixture. Allow the gelatin to bloom for 5 minutes. Cook over low heat, stirring constantly, until the gelatin completely dissolves, 5 to 10 minutes. Remove the pan from the heat and set aside to cool to room temperature. If required, strain the mixture again.

Make the berry bavarois: In a heavy-bottomed saucepan, combine the egg yolks, sugar, cornstarch, milk and vanilla. Beat with a whisk. The mixture will initially appear dry, but will become smooth upon whisking. Add ½ cup (120 ml) of the cream and whisk until smooth.

Place the saucepan over low heat and cook, whisking constantly until the mixture starts to thicken, 6 to 7 minutes. It is important to do this slowly and steadily so the eggs don't scramble and the cornstarch cooks evenly. The mixture is ready when it resembles custard and is thick enough to coat the back of a spoon.

Remove the saucepan from the heat. Add the berry puree. Mix until the bavarois is well combined.

In a separate large bowl, beat the remaining cup (240 ml) of cream into soft peaks. The cream should be thick enough to form soft shapes and just firm enough to hold briefly as you lift the whisk, then fall back into the cream. Fold the whipped cream gently into the custard mixture until well combined.

(continued)

For Assembly

28 to 30 ladyfingers

1 pint (288 g) fresh strawberries, for garnish

1 cup (148 g) fresh blueberries, for garnish

1 cup (123 g) fresh raspberries, for garnish

½ cup (69 g) fresh cherries, for garnish

Assemble: Cover the base and sides of an 8-inch (20-cm) round, 3-inch (7.5-cm)-deep springform pan with plastic wrap. Start by lining the base of the pan with ladyfingers. If there are gaps, trim the ladyfingers to fit in the gaps and use the trimmings to fill up any spaces. The base needs to be completely covered. Sprinkle 2 tablespoons (30 ml) of the simple syrup over the base.

Next, line the sides of the pan with additional ladyfingers: Trim about ½ inch (1 cm) off one end of each ladyfinger, dip the end very lightly in simple syrup and arrange them upright, trimmed end down, in a tight circle around the base.

Transfer the bavarois to the prepared pan by carefully pouring it over and between the ladyfingers. Chill in the fridge for a minimum 6 hours, preferably overnight.

When ready to serve, decorate with strawberries, blueberries, raspberries and cherries. The Berry Charlotte is best enjoyed cold.

ROCKY ROAD ICE CREAM CAKE

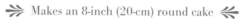 Makes an 8-inch (20-cm) round cake

Rocky road is Australia's favorite, nostalgic no-bake treat, comprising of chocolate, marshmallows and nuts. This classic, which I've reimagined as an ice cream cake, is nothing but an indulgence overload. If chocolate, nuts and marshmallows are not enough, Marzipan Fruits (page 151) are a great option to add for a fun celebration cake. Unlike other ice cream cakes, this cake will stand up to sweltering temperatures in summer because it's partly cheesecake.

Cookie Crust

Canola oil spray, for pan

25 (a scant 9 oz [250 g]) chocolate sandwich cookies, such as Oreo®

⅓ cup (76 g) unsalted butter, melted

Ice Cream Cake Filling

8 oz (225 g) cream cheese, at room temperature

½ cup (100 g) sugar

18 oz (510 g) vanilla ice cream, partially thawed

2 cups (90 g) marshmallows (use a combination of flavors)

½ cup (72 g) mixed nuts (pistachios, cashews, almonds, walnuts)

⅓ cup (67 g) glacé cherries

½ cup (84 g) chocolate chips

½ cup (62 g) fresh or frozen raspberries

Make the crust: Spray the base and sides of an 8-inch (20-cm) round, 3-inch (7.5-cm)-deep springform pan with canola oil and line the base with parchment paper. Place the springform pan on a baking sheet.

Place the cookies, including their cream filling, in a food processor and process until they resemble fine crumbs. Add the butter and process briefly until combined. Press the cookie mixture evenly over the base of the prepared pan. Chill the pan in the fridge for 30 minutes.

Make the ice cream cake filling: In a large bowl, using an electric mixer, beat together the cream cheese and sugar until light and fluffy. Add the vanilla ice cream and beat until well combined. Fold in the marshmallows, mixed nuts, glacé cherries, chocolate chips and raspberries.

Pour the filling over the cookie crust. Tap gently on the kitchen counter so the filling settles into the pan uniformly. Freeze the ice cream cake for 4 to 6 hours, preferably overnight.

(continued)

Isomalt Decoration

½ cup isomalt powder or crystals (see Note)

1 tbsp (15 ml) distilled water

1 drop pink gel food coloring

1 drop red gel food coloring (optional)

For Assembly

1 cup (45 g) regular marshmallows

¼ cup (36 g) whole roasted almonds

¼ cup (50 g) glacé cherries

8 to 10 fresh raspberries

2 tbsp (28 g) chocolate chips

NOTE: This sugar substitute can be found in cake decorating supply stores and online.

Make the isomalt decoration: In a small saucepan, combine the isomalt and water, and cook over medium heat without stirring. Bring the mixture to a boil, then lower the heat to low. Simmer until all the isomalt has melted and the mixture looks clear (not white). Remove the pan from the heat and allow the bubbles to subside before adding the food coloring.

If using one color, add the coloring and whirl the pan to allow it to blend with the isomalt mixture. If using two colors, add the second color after the previous step but do not whirl the pan. Instead, add a drop in the center of the pan, then quickly pour the isomalt onto a silicone mat. This will allow the color to flow in different directions creating a pattern. Carefully, lift up the silicone mat and tilt it so as to whirl the isomalt around while letting it cool. When it is just about to set, place the silicone mat on a tall bottle to give it a bowl shape, while allowing some of it to drip. Using clothespins to clip the mat at different places helps manipulate the direction of the drip.

You will need to do all of this quickly as isomalt sets pretty quickly. Put the shaped isomalt aside, on its mat and bottle, for 30 minutes to set. Once set, very carefully turn the mat around and peel it off the decoration. Store in an airtight container until needed.

Assemble: Place the isomalt decoration on the top of the frozen cake. Place marshmallows within and around the decoration. Decorate with almonds, glacé cherries and raspberries. Sprinkle chocolate chips all over the top. Allow the cake to sit at room temperature for 15 to 20 minutes before serving.

DRIP, DRIZZLE, POUR

This chapter is a collection of cakes that are drenched and served in syrup, poked and filled with a delicious sauce, drizzled with exquisite glazes or devilishly bathed in milky goodness.

This is arguably my favorite section in this book, in part because these techniques sound like home to me and remind me of my roots, where most desserts (such as *jalebi* or *gulab jamun* and the creamy *ras malai*) are drenched in syrup for a sensational experience. But also this a baker's best-kept secret! Cakes soaked in syrup typically remain moist and sweet right through to the center and can stay succulent and delectable for days.

Allow me to take you on a sensory journey around the globe through these cakes, from a taste of Turkey in the spellbinding, decadent Baklava Cake (page 99) to the Mexican Saffron Pistachio Tres Leches Cake (page 96) infused with Indian flavors and a fusion of cuisines that won't disappoint. Others include the fragrant, refreshing Asian-inspired Lemongrass Syrup Cake (page 95) and a luscious Spanish dulce de leche number (page 104) that is paired with coffee and cashews. The Mandarin and Fennel Seed Syrup Cake (page 91) is, by far, my favorite cake. What a remarkable difference one ingredient, like fennel seeds, can make! This cake is testimony to that.

MANDARIN AND FENNEL SEED SYRUP CAKE

≫ Makes a 10-inch (25-cm) Bundt cake ≪

This cake is pure nostalgia for me. Fennels seeds are an integral part of East Indian cuisine, where I grew up. The smell and taste takes me back to lazy school holiday mornings soaking up the sun in our balcony while the house was filled with the intoxicating aroma of *malpua*, deep-fried fennel seed dumplings that my mother was frying in the kitchen. The subtle licorice tones are enough to make this cake stand out from any regular orange-almond cake. To give the cake a showstopper look, you could garnish with Dehydrated Citrus (page 155).

Mandarin Cake

Canola oil spray, for pan

1½ cups (188 g) all-purpose flour, sifted

2 tsp (9 g) baking powder

1 cup (95 g) almond meal

4 large eggs

1 cup (200 g) sugar

¾ cup (180 ml) vegetable oil

2 tbsp (12 g) mandarin zest (from 2 to 3 mandarins, see Note)

1 cup (240 ml) fresh mandarin juice

1 tsp vanilla extract

Mandarin and Fennel Seed Syrup

1 cup (240 ml) fresh mandarin juice

1 cup (200 g) sugar

2 tbsp (18 g) fennel seeds, dry toasted

For Assembly

1 mandarin, peeled and sliced

Make the mandarin cake: Preheat the oven to 325°F (163°C). Spray a 10-inch (25-cm, 12-cup [2.8-L]) Bundt pan with canola oil.

In a medium-sized bowl, combine the flour, baking powder and almond meal.

In a large bowl, beat together the eggs and sugar until pale and fluffy, about 5 minutes. Add the oil and continue to beat until combined. Add the mandarin zest and juice and the vanilla. Beat the mixture slowly until blended.

Fold in the flour mixture until just combined. Do not overmix the batter.

Pour the batter into the prepared pan and bake for 60 to 70 minutes, or until cooked through; a skewer inserted into the middle of the cake should come out clean.

While the cake bakes, make the mandarin and fennel seed syrup: In a small saucepan, stir together the mandarin juice, sugar and fennel seeds over low heat until the sugar dissolves. Then, increase the heat to medium and boil the mixture for 10 minutes, or until the syrup thickens.

Assemble: Remove the cake from the oven and allow it to cool in the pan for 10 minutes, then run a blunt knife around the middle and the edges. Carefully turn it out onto a cake stand or plate. Pour the warm syrup over the cake. Garnish with mandarin slices.

Serve the cake warm or at room temperature.

NOTE: I used Honey Murcott mandarins, which are as sweet as honey and just beautiful to cook with. Add an extra tablespoon (15 g) of sugar if the mandarins you are using are not sweet enough.

BANANA CAKE WITH MISO CARAMEL SYRUP

If you were a kid growing up in India back in the '80s, your only option to watch the newest Bollywood film was to go to the crowded theaters or pay a high price to rent a VCR for the evening. To make the investment worthwhile, one would rent a minimum of three video cassettes. Multiply that by a good three hours per movie, and that kept us up all night. Blankets and mats were spread out on the floor for the nighttime festivity, and a bunch of bananas were kept by the doorway as refreshment. By the morning, the mound of banana skins had come to represent the snoring individuals who were falling on top of one another.

The world has evolved. Netflix and technology are available. You have banana bread, this time with miso, too. This sweet-salty cake delivers more entertainment than a Bollywood blockbuster.

Banana Topping
Canola oil spray, for pan
1 tsp white miso paste (see Note)
3 tbsp (45 ml) water, divided
½ cup (100 g) granulated sugar
3 medium-sized semi-ripe bananas

Banana Cake
½ cup (114 g) unsalted butter
¾ cup (165 g) firmly packed light or dark brown sugar
1 tsp vanilla extract
2 large eggs
2 medium-sized ripe bananas, mashed
1¼ cups (156 g) all-purpose flour
1½ tsp (6 g) baking powder
1 tsp ground cinnamon
1 tbsp (15 ml) milk

Vanilla ice cream, for serving

NOTE: Miso is a traditional Japanese seasoning paste that adds an umami touch to desserts. White miso (*shiro*) is ideal for a cake and is available in most big supermarkets, Asian stores and online.

Make the banana topping: Preheat the oven to 350°F (177°C). Spray the base and sides of an 8-inch (20-cm) round, 3-inch (7.5-cm)-deep cake pan with canola oil and line the base with parchment paper.

In a small bowl, combine the miso paste with 2 tablespoons (30 ml) of the water to loosen it.

In a small saucepan, combine the granulated sugar and remaining tablespoon (15 ml) of water. Cook over low heat until the sugar has dissolved. Bring to a boil without stirring. Increase the heat to medium and continue to cook until the mixture becomes light golden. Remove the pan from the heat and add the miso paste. The miso caramel will bubble up, but this is normal. Whirl the pan to mix evenly. Pour the miso caramel into the prepared pan.

Halve the bananas lengthwise. Place the banana halves, cut side down, over the caramel in the pan.

Make the banana cake: In a large bowl, beat together the butter, brown sugar and vanilla until pale and fluffy. Add the eggs, one at a time, beating well after each addition. Add the mashed bananas, flour, baking powder, cinnamon and milk, and beat until just combined.

Spoon the mixture over the bananas in the prepared cake pan. Spread the mixture carefully with the back of a spoon. Bake for 50 minutes, or until a skewer inserted into the middle of the cake comes out clean. Remove the cake from the oven. Set it aside for 10 minutes, then gently loosen the edges with a blunt knife. Place a wire rack over a baking sheet to catch the drips. Carefully turn out the cake onto the wire rack.

Serve warm or at room temperature with a side of vanilla ice cream.

LEMONGRASS SYRUP CAKE

Lemongrass is so underrated in desserts. Treat your palate to the refreshing taste of this aromatic herb with generous helpings of sticky, sweet syrup. The addition of coconut and lime takes you on a journey to South East Asia.

Lemongrass Cake

Canola oil spray, for pan

¾ cup (180 ml) milk

2 stalks (30 g) lemongrass, chopped roughly

½ cup (114 g) unsalted butter, at room temperature

1 cup (200 g) sugar

3 large eggs

1 tsp freshly grated lime zest

1¼ cups (156 g) self-rising flour

1¼ cups (113 g) desiccated coconut

Lime and Lemongrass Syrup

⅓ cup (80 ml) water

¼ cup (60 ml) fresh lime juice

¼ cup (50 g) sugar

1 lemongrass stalk (15 g), chopped finely

1 tsp finely grated lime zest

Vanilla ice cream, for serving

Make the lemongrass cake: Preheat the oven to 350°F (177°C). Spray the base and sides of a 9-inch (23-cm) round, 3-inch (7.5-cm)-deep cake pan with canola oil and line the base with parchment paper.

Using a blender or food processor, blend together the milk and lemongrass. Set aside for 10 minutes to infuse. Strain, discarding the lemongrass residue and reserving the milk for later.

In a large bowl, beat together the butter and sugar until pale and fluffy. Add the eggs, one at a time, beating well after each addition. Beat in the lime zest.

Fold in the flour and coconut, alternating with the lemongrass-infused milk, until well combined.

Transfer the batter to the prepared pan. Bake for 40 to 45 minutes, or until a skewer inserted into the middle of the cake comes out clean. Remove the pan from the oven. Set it aside for 10 minutes, then gently run a blunt knife around the edges to loosen the cake. Carefully turn it out onto a serving plate or cake stand. Using a skewer, poke holes in the surface of the cake while it's still warm.

Make the lime and lemongrass syrup: In a medium-sized saucepan, combine the water, lime juice, sugar, lemongrass and lime zest. Cook the mixture over medium heat until it comes to a boil. Lower the heat to low and simmer for 5 to 7 minutes, or until the mixture has thickened slightly. Based on your preference, you could strain the syrup to remove the solid bits, or just use it as is.

Assemble: Pour the hot syrup over the cake while it is still warm. Allow the cake to cool slightly before slicing. The cake is best served with a side of vanilla ice cream.

SAFFRON PISTACHIO TRES LECHES CAKE

In the kitchen, there are times when "milk" turns into "silk." How do I know this? I grew up in a place where milk or dairy is the backbone of sweet treats. The land of the well-known ras malai, a devilishly delicious clotted cream dumpling, immersed in a sumptuous bath of thickened, flavored milk. Consider this to be a magnified version of ras malai: a light sponge cake flavored with saffron, rose, cardamom and pistachios, replete with creamy deliciousness from three kinds of milk, which this cake gets its name from. It is such a delight to give this Mexican classic an Indian touch.

Sponge Cake

Canola oil spray, for pan

1 cup (125 g) all-purpose flour

¼ cup (32 g) cornstarch

⅓ cup (80 ml) boiling water

2 tbsp (28 g) unsalted butter, at room temperature

4 large eggs, at room temperature

¾ cup (150 g) sugar

Milk Sauce

½ tsp saffron threads

¾ cup (180 ml) evaporated milk

1 can (395 g) sweetened condensed milk

½ cup (120 ml) heavy cream

For Assembly

1 cup (240 ml) heavy cream, whipped to stiff peaks

¼ cup (25 g) chopped pistachios, for garnish

¼ cup (10 g) dried edible rosebuds and rose petals, for garnish

Make the sponge cake: Preheat the oven to 350°F (177°C). Lightly spray the base and sides of an 8-inch (20-cm) square, 3-inch (7.5-cm)-deep cake pan with canola oil

In a medium-sized bowl, sift the flour and cornstarch twice. In a small cup or bowl, combine the boiling water and butter. Set aside to cool.

In a large bowl, beat the eggs until light and fluffy. Add the sugar and continue to beat until tripled in volume, 7 to 8 minutes. The mixture should look thick and fall back in thick ribbons when the beaters are lifted.

Gently fold the flour mixture into the egg mixture, then fold in the butter mixture. Do this gradually so as to not deflate the batter too much.

Transfer the batter to the prepared pan and smooth out the surface with a spatula. Bake for 40 to 45 minutes, or until the sponge starts to pull away from the sides and springs back when lightly touched.

Remove the pan from the oven. Allow the cake to cool for 10 minutes.

While the cake bakes, make the milk sauce: In a medium-sized microwave-safe bowl, combine the saffron threads and evaporated milk. Microwave for 30 seconds, or until warm. Set the mixture aside for 15 minutes for the saffron to infuse.

Add the condensed milk and cream, and stir to combine.

Assemble: Once the cake has cooled for 10 minutes, using a skewer, poke holes in the surface of the cake. Slowly pour the milk sauce uniformly over the cake. Cover and chill the pan in the fridge for at least 4 hours, preferably overnight.

Spread the whipped cream evenly over the cake. Sprinkle with the chopped pistachios, rosebuds and rose petals. Refrigerate until ready to serve. The cake is best enjoyed cold or at room temperature.

BAKLAVA CAKE

Makes an 8-inch (20-cm) round cake

Immerse your senses in a rippling sea of flavor and texture with this scrumptiously rich and sweet baklava cake. If you're a fan of the traditional baklava, you will concur that the process of making it is fascinating. This one is less intricate. The baklava cake arguably gets better over time as it allows the honey syrup to work its magic through the cake.

Baklava Cake

Canola oil spray, for pan

½ cup (50 g) chopped pistachios

⅓ cup (39 g) chopped walnuts

1 cup (125 g) self-rising flour

1 tsp ground cinnamon

1 tsp ground cardamom

½ cup (114 g) unsalted butter, at room temperature

1 cup (200 g) sugar

1 tbsp (15 ml) rose water

2 large eggs

½ cup (120 ml) Greek yogurt

⅓ cup (80 ml) milk

Honey Syrup

⅓ cup (80 ml) water

½ cup (100 g) sugar

⅓ cup (80 ml) honey

1 tsp fresh lemon juice

For Garnish

2 tbsp (14 g) chopped pistachios

2 tbsp (4 g) dried edible rose petals

Make the baklava cake: Preheat the oven to 350°F (177°C). Spray the base and sides of an 8-inch (20-cm) round, 3-inch (7.5-cm)-deep cake pan with canola oil and line the base with parchment paper.

In a food processor, process or pulse the pistachio and walnuts together until you have a mixture of fine crumbs as well as some small pieces of nuts. In a medium-sized bowl, combine the flour, nut mixture, cinnamon and cardamom and stir together well.

In a large bowl, beat together the butter and sugar until light and fluffy. Add the rose water and then add the eggs, one at a time, beating well after each addition. Fold in the flour mixture, alternating with the yogurt and milk, until well combined.

Transfer the batter to the prepared pan. Bake for 55 to 60 minutes, or until the cake turns golden brown and a skewer inserted into the middle of the cake comes out clean. Remove the pan from the oven. Set it aside for 10 minutes, then gently run a blunt knife around the edges to loosen the cake. Carefully turn it out onto a wire rack to cool slightly. Using a skewer, poke holes in the cake while still warm.

While the cake cools, make the honey syrup: In a small saucepan, combine the water, sugar, honey and lemon juice. Bring to a boil over medium-high heat, stirring frequently until the sugar dissolves. Lower the heat to low and continue to simmer until the syrup thickens, 4 to 5 minutes. Remove from the heat and allow the syrup to cool slightly. It will thicken further upon cooling.

Assemble: Pour the warm syrup over the warm cake. Decorate the edges with chopped pistachios and dried rose petals. The cake is best enjoyed warm or at room temperature.

PASSION FRUIT BURNT BASQUE CHEESECAKE

⇝ Makes an 8-inch (20-cm) round cake ⇜

Burnt Basque cheesecakes have been very trendy in the last few years and for good reason. Crust-free, with a golden, caramelized exterior and a soft, creamy center, this is one cheesecake that begs to be burnt, cracked and baked at high temperatures. Which also implies that this cheesecake is hard to mess up. The presence of passion fruit puree, which makes it seductively aromatic, acidic, and crunchy from the seeds, brings out the tropical flavors in this dish.

Canola oil spray, for pan

2⅔ cups (620 g) cream cheese, at room temperature

4 large eggs, at room temperature

1¼ cups (250 g) sugar

1¼ cups (300 ml) heavy cream

¾ cup (180 ml) passion fruit puree, divided

1 tbsp (8 g) all-purpose flour

Preheat the oven to 400°F (204°C). Spray the base and sides of an 8-inch (20-cm) round, 3-inch (7.5-cm)-deep springform pan with canola oil and line the base and sides with parchment paper. Allow the sheets of parchment paper to overlap, making sure the paper that lines the sides extends at least ¾ inch (2 cm) above the rim of the pan. Place the pan on a baking sheet.

Using an electric mixer, beat the cream cheese until smooth and creamy. Add the eggs, one at a time, beating well after each addition. Gradually beat in the sugar, then the cream and ¼ cup (60 ml) of the passion fruit puree. Using a fine-mesh sieve, sift the flour over the cream cheese mixture, and beat until just incorporated.

Pour the batter into the prepared pan. Tap the pan gently on a flat surface to remove any air bubbles. Bake for 65 to 75 minutes, or until the top is dark brown and center is still wobbly.

Remove the cheesecake from the oven. Allow it to cool completely in the pan, then carefully remove the springform ring and gently peel away the parchment paper from the sides of the cheesecake. Drizzle with the remaining ½ cup (120 ml) of passion fruit puree. Slice into wedges and enjoy at room temperature or cold from the fridge.

BLUEBERRY COCONUT POKE CAKE

This cake makes me so happy. It reminds me of the joy of browsing through my mother's lavish sari collection as a kid. She was in possession of a sizable number of purple ones. Who knows, maybe one of them served as inspiration for this dessert! Or maybe it's the excitement of poking holes in a cake and stuffing it with a delectable surprise that you can only discover when you cut through it.

Blueberry Sauce

2 cups (296 g) blueberries, fresh or frozen

1 tsp fresh lemon juice

2 tbsp (26 g) granulated sugar

2 tbsp (30 ml) water

Blueberry Coconut Cake

Canola oil spray, for pan

⅔ cup (152 g) unsalted butter

1 cup (200 g) granulated sugar

2 large eggs

1 cup (240 ml) Greek yogurt

1 tsp vanilla extract

1½ cups (188 g) self-rising flour

½ cup (45 g) desiccated coconut

¼ cup (60 ml) whole milk

Blueberry Cream Cheese Frosting

8 oz (226 g) cream cheese, at room temperature

½ cup (114 g) unsalted butter, at room temperature

2 cups (240 g) powdered sugar

¼ cup (60 ml) blueberry sauce

For Garnish

1 cup (148 g) fresh blueberries

Edible viola flowers

Make the blueberry sauce: In a small saucepan, combine the blueberries, lemon juice, granulated sugar and water over low heat. Bring to a boil, stirring constantly, until the blueberries soften and the mixture is thick. Using the back of a spoon, lightly crush the blueberries for a puree-like consistency.

Make the blueberry coconut cake: Preheat the oven to 350°F (177°C). Spray the base and sides of an 8-inch (20-cm) square, 3-inch (7.5-cm)-deep cake pan with canola oil and line the base with parchment paper.

In a large bowl, beat together the butter and granulated sugar until pale and fluffy. Add the eggs, one at a time, beating well after each addition. Beat in the yogurt and vanilla. Fold in the flour and coconut, alternately with the milk, until just combined.

Transfer the mixture to the prepared pan. Bake for 60 to 65 minutes, or until a skewer inserted into the middle of the cake comes out clean. Remove the cake from the oven. Set it aside for 5 minutes, then carefully turn it out onto a wire rack. Set the cake aside for 15 minutes.

Using the round handle of a wooden spoon, poke holes into the cake at 1¼-inch (3-cm) intervals. Reserving ¼ cup (60 ml) for the frosting, spoon the remaining blueberry sauce into the holes. Set the cake aside to cool completely before frosting.

While the cake cools, make the blueberry cream cheese frosting: In a large bowl, using a hand mixer or stand mixer, beat together the cream cheese and butter until smooth and creamy. Add the powdered sugar, ½ cup (60 g) at a time, beating well after each addition, until smooth. Add the reserved blueberry sauce and beat for 1 minute, or until well blended.

Assemble: Place the cake on a serving plate or tray. Spread the top of the cake with the blueberry cream cheese frosting. Decorate with fresh blueberries and edible flowers. Slice and serve.

DULCE DE LECHE AND COFFEE-GLAZED CASHEW CAKE

Makes an 8-inch (20-cm) round cake

I knew as soon as I made this cake that it would be added to my repertoire of go-to cakes. Drip, drizzle or pour, but don't scrimp on the dulce de leche. The coffee-glazed cashews are the pièce de résistance in the cake. Although you can't help but eat each component by itself, if you have the patience, the whole cake is even better than the sum of its parts.

Dulce de Leche Cake
Canola oil spray, for pan
1¼ cups (156 g) self-rising flour
¼ cup (31 g) all-purpose flour
1 tbsp (7 g) ground cinnamon
¾ cup (170 g) unsalted butter, at room temperature
¾ cup (150 g) sugar
2 large eggs
1 tsp vanilla extract
½ cup (120 ml) milk

Coffee-Glazed Cashews
1 tbsp (15 ml) water
½ tsp instant coffee powder
1 tbsp (15 ml) honey
3 tbsp (39 g) sugar
1 cup (146 g) cashews

For Assembly
½ cup (112 g) dulce de leche (store-bought or homemade)

Make the dulce de leche cake: Preheat the oven to 340°F (171°C). Spray the base and sides of an 8-inch (20-cm) round, 3-inch (7.5-cm)-deep cake pan with canola oil and line the base with parchment paper.

Into a medium-sized bowl, sift the self-rising flour, all-purpose flour and cinnamon. Stir them together and set the bowl aside until needed.

In a large bowl, beat together the butter and sugar until pale and fluffy. Add the eggs, one at a time, beating well after each addition. Beat in the vanilla.

Fold in the flour mixture, alternating with the milk, until just combined.

Transfer the batter to the prepared cake pan. Bake for 50 to 55 minutes, or until a skewer inserted into the middle of the cake comes out clean. Remove the cake from the oven. Set it aside for 10 minutes, then gently run a blunt knife around the edges to loosen the cake. Carefully turn it out onto a wire rack to cool completely.

Make the coffee-glazed cashews: Preheat the oven to 350°F (177°C). Line a baking sheet with parchment paper.

In a small saucepan, combine the water, coffee powder, honey and sugar. Cook over medium heat, stirring frequently, until the sugar is dissolved. Remove the pan from the heat, then add the cashews. Give the mixture a good stir until all the nuts are evenly coated.

Spread the cashew mixture in a single layer on the prepared baking sheet. Bake for 5 minutes, then stir. Bake for another 10 minutes. Remove from the oven and allow the nuts to cool completely on the baking sheet. Break into small pieces and store in an airtight container until needed.

Assemble: In a microwave-safe bowl, microwave the dulce de leche for 8 to 10 seconds to lighten it. Give it a good stir. Pour it over the top of the cake, allowing some to drip off the edges. Allow to set for about 10 minutes, then decorate the top with the coffee-glazed cashews. The cake is best enjoyed at room temperature or slightly warm.

BLOOD ORANGE CAKE WITH GINGER DRIZZLE

~ Makes an 8-inch (20-cm) round cake ~

Simple, moreish and with a zingy taste, this cake embraces everything we love about blood oranges. From its distinctive sweet-tart flavor to its deep crimson hue. The cake is elevated with a drizzle of melted, ginger-flavored white chocolate. If blood oranges are not in season, regular oranges can be used and the cake can be decorated with dehydrated blood orange slices (page 155) for a classy touch.

Blood Orange Cake
Canola oil spray, for pan

1 cup (227 g) unsalted butter, at room temperature

1 cup (200 g) sugar

1 tbsp (6 g) blood orange zest

4 large eggs

1⅔ cups (208 g) self-rising flour

½ cup (120 ml) fresh blood orange juice

White Chocolate Flower
3.5 oz (100 g) white chocolate, chopped finely

White Chocolate Ginger Drizzle
3.5 oz (100 g) white chocolate, chopped finely

1 tsp ground ginger

For Garnish
1 blood orange, sliced thinly

NOTE: These days, silicone molds are widely available in a variety of sizes and shapes at eBay, Amazon, Etsy and cake decorating stores. Your cakes and sweets will have more height and flair thanks to this simple investment.

Make the blood orange cake: Preheat the oven to 350°F (177°C). Spray the base and sides of an 8-inch (20-cm) round, 3-inch (7.5-cm)-deep cake pan with canola oil and line the base with parchment paper.

In a large bowl, beat together the butter, sugar and blood orange zest until pale and fluffy. Add the eggs, one at a time, beating well after each addition.

Using a spatula, fold the flour into the butter mixture until well combined. Fold in the blood orange juice until just combined.

Pour the batter into the prepared pan and smooth out the surface with the spatula or the back of a spoon. Bake for 45 to 50 minutes, or until a skewer inserted into the middle of the cake comes out clean. Remove the cake from the oven. Set it aside for 5 minutes, then carefully turn it out onto a wire rack.

Make the white chocolate flower: In a microwave-safe bowl, microwave the white chocolate pieces on low for 20 seconds, then remove and stir. Return the bowl to the microwave and repeat the process until all the chocolate has melted and has turned into a smooth liquid. Alternatively, the chocolate can be melted in a heatproof bowl that is placed over a saucepan of simmering water (make sure the bottom of the bowl doesn't touch the water).

Spoon the chocolate carefully into a 2¾-inch (7-cm)-wide silicone rose mold that is placed on a small baking sheet or plate for ease of movement into the fridge. Chill in the fridge to set, about 30 minutes. Then, gently unmold and store in an airtight container in the fridge until needed.

Make the white chocolate drizzle: In a microwave-safe bowl, microwave the white chocolate pieces on low for 20 seconds, then remove and stir. Return the bowl to the microwave and repeat the process until all the chocolate has melted into a smooth liquid. Add the ginger and mix well.

Assemble: Once the cake has cooled to room temperature, drizzle the melted chocolate on top, allowing some of it to trickle down the sides. Decorate the edges with blood orange slices. Place the white chocolate flower on the top. Slice and serve.

lie in wait when you allow your culinary curiosity to stray through the sweeter side of botanical ingredients.

Edible botanicals, including herbs and flowers, are becoming increasingly popular due to their sustainability, natural flavors and ability to tap into health and wellness. Just a few years ago, flowers in particular were considered a "premium" ingredient. Today, they are readily accessible and cater to the rising demand for food that provides a sensory experience.

On the other hand, we use a variety of herbs in our daily lives that haven't yet reached their full potential as components in desserts. Everyday herbs, such as basil, mint and rosemary, can be used in innovative ways to enliven cakes or add a pop of refreshing color, and are perhaps a clever way of "eating your greens."

In this chapter, I've paired botanicals with flavors that make them shine. The Pistachio Cake with Rose Petal Jam (page 115) is a walk down memory lane for me. Once you've tasted it, this beautiful jam will undoubtedly grace your kitchen for life. A mouthwatering combination is the Rich Chocolate Cake with Mint Caramel (page 125). Lemon and basil go together like wine and cheese. Top that pairing with meringue, and you have a divine Lemon Basil Meringue Cake (page 112) that people are never going to forget. The Apricot and Chamomile Cake (page 116) is usually my little tease for those attempting to guess what that underlying delicate flavor is as they make their way through the vibrant, luscious fruit.

Be it for romantic evenings, important holidays or entertaining guests, these cakes are great to make at home and can leave a lasting impression.

ROSE WATER AND POMEGRANATE CAKE

≫ Makes an 8-inch (20-cm) round cake ≪

I had a love-hate relationship with pomegranate when I was younger. Alongside papayas, they were the most eaten fruit at home. My mother and her sisters firmly believed that, for a teenager, it was the key to radiant skin and possibly the secret to finding a compatible partner for the future. I can't guarantee the outcome; however, pomegranates are the most exquisite ingredient to use and photograph. In my pantry, I have more bottles of rose water than I do of vanilla extract. It goes without saying that I absolutely adore this cake, and I have employed this flavor combination in a number of desserts in the past.

Rose Water Cake

Canola oil spray, for pan

½ cup (114 g) unsalted butter, softened

1 cup (200 g) granulated sugar

2 large eggs

1 tbsp (15 ml) rose water

1½ cups (188 g) self-rising flour, sifted

½ cup (63 g) all-purpose flour, sifted

1¼ cups (300 ml) sour cream

¼ cup (60 ml) milk

½ cup (50 g) chopped pistachios

Ricotta Frosting

¼ cup (58 g) cream cheese, at room temperature

½ cup (123 g) firm ricotta cheese, at room temperature

¼ cup (60 ml) heavy cream

1 cup (120 g) powdered sugar

½ tsp ground cardamom, or 1 tsp vanilla extract

For Garnish

½ cup (78 g) pomegranate arils

2 tbsp (14 g) chopped pistachios

Edible dried rosebuds or rose petals (optional)

Make the rose water cake: Preheat the oven to 325°F (163°C). Spray the base and sides of an 8-inch (20-cm) round, 3-inch (7.5-cm)-deep cake pan with canola oil and line the base with parchment paper.

In a large bowl, beat together the butter and granulated sugar until light and fluffy, about 5 minutes. Add the eggs, one at a time, beating well after each addition. Add the rose water and beat for 20 seconds.

Using a large metal spoon, fold in the self-rising flour and all-purpose flour, along with the sour cream and milk, in alternating batches until well combined. Do not overmix the batter. Fold in the chopped pistachios.

Pour the batter into the prepared cake pan. Smooth the surface with a spatula or the back of a spoon. Bake for 90 to 95 minutes, or until a skewer inserted into the middle of the cake comes out clean. Remove the cake from the oven and allow to rest in the pan for 10 minutes. Gently turn it out onto a wire rack to cool.

Make the ricotta frosting: In a medium-sized bowl, using an electric mixer, beat the cream cheese until pale and fluffy, about 2 minutes. Add the ricotta, cream, powdered sugar and cardamom, then beat on high speed until the mixture starts to look thick and holds soft peaks, 4 to 5 minutes.

Assemble: Dollop the frosting on the cooled cake. Sprinkle the top with pomegranate arils and chopped pistachios. Decorate the top with edible rosebuds or petals (if using). Store the cake, covered, in the fridge. When ready to serve, allow to sit at room temperature for at least 30 minutes.

LEMON BASIL MERINGUE CAKE

Ah, the sweet scent of basil! Since I started experimenting with herbal sweets, a basil panna cotta tart has been my all-time favorite. Since then, I've had the notion to include fresh basil into a cake recipe. It did not let me down in the least. The cake is nicely finished with a torched meringue and a layer of freshness provided by the lemon basil syrup.

Lemon Basil Cake

Canola oil spray, for pan

¾ cup (150 g) sugar

1 tbsp (6 g) lemon zest

3 tbsp (5 g) finely chopped fresh basil

3 large eggs

1 tbsp (15 ml) fresh lemon juice

¾ cup (180 ml) Greek yogurt

⅓ cup (80 ml) extra virgin olive oil

1½ cups (188 g) self-rising flour

Lemon Basil Syrup (see Notes)

¼ cup (60 ml) fresh lemon juice

1 tbsp (2 g) large fresh basil leaves (about 3 or 4)

1 tbsp (13 g) sugar

Meringue

3 large egg whites

½ cup (100 g) sugar

Make the lemon basil cake: Preheat the oven to 350°F (177°C). Spray the base and sides of an 8-inch (20-cm) round, 3-inch (7.5-cm)-deep cake pan with canola oil and line the base with parchment paper.

In a large bowl, beat together the sugar, lemon zest and basil, about 1 minute. Add the eggs, one at a time, beating well after each addition. Add the lemon juice, yogurt and olive oil, and beat until well combined. Fold in the flour until just combined.

Transfer the batter to the prepared pan. Bake for 40 to 45 minutes, or until a skewer inserted into the middle of the cake comes out clean. Remove the pan from the oven. Set it aside for 10 minutes, then gently run a blunt knife around the edges to loosen the cake. Carefully turn it out onto a wire rack to cool slightly. Using a skewer, poke holes into the cake while still warm.

While the cake cools slightly, make the lemon basil syrup: In a small saucepan, combine the lemon juice, basil and sugar. Cook over medium heat for 5 minutes, or until slightly thickened. Discard the basil leaves.

Drizzle the syrup over the warm cake. Set the cake aside to cool completely.

Make the meringue: In a clean, dry large bowl, using an electric mixer, beat the egg whites until soft peaks appear. Gradually, add the sugar, 1 tablespoon (15 g) at a time, beating constantly, until the sugar dissolves and the meringue is thick and glossy, 5 to 6 minutes.

Assemble: Using the back of a spoon, spread the meringue over the cooled cake, doming it in the center and creating large swirls around it. Using a kitchen torch, caramelize the meringue edges. If you do not have a kitchen torch, you can enjoy the cake without the meringue.

NOTES: The lemon basil syrup can be skipped if you are in a hurry, but it adds an extra punch of flavor and moisture to the cake.

Candied basil (page 152) would make a great garnish for this cake.

PISTACHIO CAKE WITH ROSE PETAL JAM

I recently read an article titled "Five Ways to Apologize to Your Significant Other." There is a sixth option, though, that I can attest to being a successful means of making apologies if you have erred. Make this beyond-exquisite pistachio cake topped with ample amounts of rose petal jam.

Indian cuisine has always used roses as a key ingredient in recipes. Today rose water and rose petal jam are popular all over the world. Is there anything more seductive, romantic and intoxicating than eating a meal of roses? Traditionally, fresh organic rose petals are used to make this jam, but for simplicity's sake, I chose to use dried edible rose petals. This cake is ideal for Mother's Day, Valentine's Day or any other important occasion.

Rose Petal Jam

1 cup (240 ml) water

1 cup (200 g) sugar

1 cup (20 g) dried edible rose petals

1 tsp fresh lemon juice

1 tbsp (15 ml) rose water

Pistachio Cake

Canola oil spray, for pan

1¼ cups (156 g) self-rising flour

1 tsp baking powder

1¾ cups (175 g) ground pistachios

¾ cup (170 g) unsalted butter, at room temperature

1 cup (200 g) sugar

4 large eggs

1 tsp rose water

¼ cup (60 ml) milk

2 tbsp (14 g) chopped pistachios, for garnish

Unsprayed rose, for garnish

Make the rose petal jam: In a medium-sized saucepan over medium heat, combine the water and sugar and cook until the sugar has dissolved. Add the dried rose petals and lemon juice. Lower the heat to low and continue to cook, stirring frequently, about 10 minutes. Once the mixture has thickened and the petals have almost disintegrated, remove from the heat and add the rose water. Allow to cool in the pan, then transfer to an airtight container or Mason jar and refrigerate until needed.

Make the pistachio cake: Preheat the oven to 350°F (177°C). Spray the base and sides of an 8-inch (20-cm) round, 3-inch (7.5-cm)-deep cake pan with canola oil and line the base with parchment paper.

In a medium-sized bowl, stir together the flour, baking powder and ground pistachios.

In a large bowl, beat together the butter and sugar until pale and fluffy. Add the eggs, one at a time, beating well after each addition.

Add the flour mixture, rose water and milk. Beat until well combined.

Transfer the batter to the prepared cake pan. Bake for 60 to 65 minutes, or until a skewer inserted into the middle of the cake comes out clean. Remove the cake from the oven. Set it aside for 10 minutes, then gently run a blunt knife around the edges to loosen the cake. Carefully turn it out onto a wire rack to cool completely.

Assemble: Place the cooled cake on a cake plate or serving stand. Spread 3 tablespoons (45 ml) of the rose petal jam over the top of the cake. Sprinkle with chopped pistachios. Cover the base and/or stem of a rose with parchment paper and place on top of the cake.

APRICOT AND CHAMOMILE CAKE

When you are feeling down and depressed, you don't need to empty your pockets to different getaways and therapies. Consider trying this chamomile tea–infused apricot cake. The lovely, flowery scent of chamomile blossoms is incredibly calming. Studded with plump, juicy apricots, this cake is something else!

½ cup (120 ml) milk

2 chamomile tea bags

Canola oil spray, for pan

¾ cup (170 g) unsalted butter, at room temperature

¾ cup (150 g) granulated sugar

3 large eggs

1½ cups (188 g) self-rising flour

1 cup (95 g) almond meal

6 apricots, halved and pitted

Powdered sugar, for dusting

Dried chamomile flowers, for garnish (optional; see Notes)

In a small saucepan, heat the milk over low heat until it reaches a simmer. Remove from the heat and place the tea bags in the milk. Allow the tea bags to infuse for 30 minutes. Press the tea bags with the back of a spoon to extract more flavor from them. Discard the tea bags and set the milk aside to cool to room temperature.

Preheat the oven to 350°F (177°C). Spray the base and sides of a 9-inch (23-cm) round, 3-inch (7.5-cm)-deep cake pan with canola oil and line the base with parchment paper.

In a large bowl, beat together the butter and granulated sugar until pale and fluffy. Add the eggs, one at a time, beating well after each addition.

Fold in the flour and the almond meal, alternating with the milk, until just combined. Transfer the batter to the prepared cake pan. Smooth the surface with the back of a spoon and arrange the apricot halves, cut side up, over the surface of the batter.

Bake for 60 to 65 minutes, or until a skewer inserted into the middle of the cake comes out clean. Remove the cake from the oven. Set it aside for 10 minutes, then gently run a blunt knife around the edges to loosen the cake. Carefully turn it out onto a wire rack to cool completely.

Once cooled down, dust with powdered sugar and garnish with dried chamomile flowers (if using).

NOTES: Chamomile tea bags are available in all major supermarkets. Dried chamomile flowers are usually available in health and wellness stores, Amazon and eBay. Some tea stores also stock them.

If apricots are not in season, replace them with sliced pears, persimmons or even strawberries, keeping in mind that the fruit you use should be similar or lighter in weight and size, or they could sink to the bottom.

LAVENDER LOVER'S CAKE

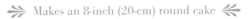

There are three categories of lavender lovers. Some adore the scent, while others love the pretty purple color and there are those who are taken by the earthy, refreshing flavor. Which group do you belong to? Perhaps, like me, you are all three, in which case this cake is for you: a celebration of lavender's flavor, aroma and color. To get the best out of culinary lavender, we first make lavender sugar, a simple step that ensures your cake is every bit lavender-ish and delicious in every bite.

Lavender Cake

Canola oil spray, for pan

¾ cup (150 g) granulated sugar

1 tbsp (8 g) culinary dried lavender

1¼ cups (156 g) self-rising flour

¼ cup (31 g) all-purpose flour

¾ cup (170 g) unsalted butter, at room temperature

2 large eggs

½ cup (120 ml) milk

Vanilla Buttercream

1 cup (227 g) unsalted butter, at room temperature

4 cups (480 g) powdered sugar

1 tsp vanilla extract

3 tbsp (45 ml) whole milk

4 drops purple gel food coloring

Make the lavender cake: Preheat the oven to 350°F (177°C). Spray the base and sides of an 8-inch (20-cm) round, 3-inch (7.5-cm)-deep cake pan with canola oil and line the base with parchment paper.

In a food processor, process the granulated sugar and lavender until the lavender has broken down and blended with the sugar.

Into a medium-sized bowl, sift the self-rising and all-purpose flours. Stir them together and set the bowl aside until needed.

In a large bowl, beat together the butter and lavender sugar until pale and fluffy. Add the eggs, one at a time, beating well after each addition. Fold in the flour mixture, alternating with the milk, until just combined.

Transfer the batter to the prepared cake pan. Bake for 40 to 45 minutes, or until a skewer inserted into the middle of the cake comes out clean. Remove the cake from the oven. Set it aside for 10 minutes, then gently run a blunt knife around the edges to loosen the cake. Carefully turn it out onto a wire rack to cool completely.

Make the vanilla buttercream: In a large bowl, using an electric mixer, beat the butter until light and fluffy, 2 to 3 minutes. Add the powdered sugar, a little at a time, beating constantly until well combined, scraping down the sides of the bowl as and when required. Add the vanilla and milk, and beat until smooth.

(continued)

Assemble: Divide the buttercream equally among three small bowls. Leave the first bowl as is. To the second bowl, add one drop of purple food coloring, or more if you desire a brighter color. Blend until no white streaks appear. To the third bowl add more color, two or three drops, and blend until smooth.

Using a piping bag fitted with an open star nozzle, working with one color of buttercream at a time, pipe rosettes onto the cake in an ombré effect, starting from the uncolored buttercream in the center, then the lighter color and finally the brighter color.

NOTES: Culinary dried lavender is easily available in health and wellness stores, as well as online at Amazon, eBay and Etsy. While it may seem like a small investment, I can assure you it's worth it. It lasts a while and its usage is diverse, ranging from syrups for cocktails, desserts and even coffee.

Let me share a secret way of using it on a frequent basis: lavender sugar, made simply by adding the culinary dried lavender to granulated sugar and storing in an airtight container. This sugar can then be added to your favorite beverage, yogurt and my favorite, whipped cream. Guests are blown away every single time!

ROSEMARY CRUSTED CRANBERRY CHEESECAKE

For a holiday treat, rosemary and cranberries are unbeatable. Since it can be made in advance, this cheesecake is ideal for Christmas. Dried cranberries are an excellent alternative if you wish to create this cake at any time of the year. Plus, fresh or frozen cranberries are difficult to acquire and almost unavailable in Australia. The mix of tangy cranberries and earthy rosemary is remarkable in this creamy cheesecake. Slices of Dehydrated Citrus (page 155) are another way of garnishing it for a festive feel.

Cheesecake Crust

Canola oil spray, for pan

5 oz (150 g) graham crackers or digestive biscuits

1 tbsp (2 g) fresh rosemary leaves

⅓ cup (76 g) unsalted butter

Cheesecake Filling

½ cup (120 ml) milk

1 tbsp (9 g) powdered gelatin

11 oz (312 g) cream cheese, at room temperature

¾ cup (150 g) sugar

1 cup (240 ml) heavy cream

1 tsp vanilla extract

Make the cheesecake crust: Spray the base and sides of an 8-inch (20-cm) round, 3-inch (7.5-cm)-deep springform pan with canola oil and line the base with parchment paper. Place the springform pan on a baking sheet for ease of movement, in and out of the fridge.

In a food processor, combine the graham crackers and rosemary leaves and process until they resemble fine crumbs. The leaves will look as if they have been finely shredded. Add the butter and process briefly until combined. Press the mixture evenly over the base of the prepared pan. Chill the pan in the fridge for 30 minutes.

Make the cheesecake filling: Pour the milk into a small saucepan and sprinkle the gelatin over it. Allow the gelatin to bloom for 5 minutes. Cook the milk over low heat, stirring constantly, until the gelatin dissolves (do not boil). Remove from the heat and allow to cool to room temperature.

In a large bowl, beat together the cream cheese and sugar until the mixture is smooth and creamy. Add the cream and vanilla, and continue to beat until well blended and fluffy. Add the gelatin mixture and beat until just combined. Pour the filling over the crust. Chill the cheesecake in the fridge for 4 to 6 hours, preferably overnight.

(continued)

Cranberry and Rosemary Sauce

¾ cup (90 g) dried cranberries
(see Note)

½ cup (120 ml) naturally sweetened
cranberry juice

2 tbsp (26 g) sugar

1 tsp freshly grated orange zest

1 tbsp (2 g) fresh rosemary leaves

2 tbsp (30 ml) water

1 tbsp (8 g) cornstarch

For Garnish

Meringue Kisses (page 156)

Candied rosemary leaves (page 152)

Make the cranberry sauce: In a medium-sized saucepan, combine the dried cranberries, cranberry juice, sugar, orange zest and rosemary leaves. Bring to a boil over medium heat, 3 to 4 minutes. Lower the heat to low and continue to simmer until the cranberries start to plump up slightly, 3 to 5 minutes.

In a small bowl, stir together the water and cornstarch. Add the mixture to the cranberry sauce in the pan. Stir constantly and allow to cook until the sauce thickens, 1 to 2 minutes. Remove the pan from the heat. Transfer the sauce to a heatproof bowl and allow to cool before using.

Assemble: Once the cheesecake has set nicely, spread the cranberry sauce over the top of the filling. Decorate with meringue kisses and candied rosemary leaves.

NOTE: The sauce can be made with fresh or frozen cranberries. Unfortunately, in Australia, we don't have access to these from regular stores, so I found a way to use dried cranberries. If you're using fresh ones, reduce the quantity to ½ cup (50 g); if using frozen, use ½ cup (55 g).

RICH CHOCOLATE CAKE WITH MINT CARAMEL

≫ Makes an 8-inch (20-cm) round cake ≪

Can we take a moment to appreciate mint for improving our meals and our lives? Salads, marinades, cocktails, dessert garnishes and much more. Fresh mint leaves used to flavor a cake or dessert are uncommon, though. When you do use them, I guarantee you'll want to toss the bottle of peppermint extract. Mint gives the praline, which is subsequently broken up and put to the frosting, a tremendous amount of freshness. The dense chocolate cake contrasts wonderfully with the mint as well. You can expect a real flavor explosion!

Rich Chocolate Cake

Canola oil spray, for pan

⅔ cup (152 g) unsalted butter, cubed

5.5 oz (150 g) dark chocolate, chopped

1 cup (220 g) firmly packed light or dark brown sugar

½ cup (120 ml) cold water

2 large eggs, lightly beaten

1 cup (125 g) all-purpose flour

⅔ cup (83 g) self-rising flour

2 tbsp (11 g) unsweetened cocoa powder

Mint caramel shards (page 159)

Chocolate Cream Cheese Frosting

4 oz (115 g) cream cheese, at room temperature

¼ cup (57 g) unsalted butter, at room temperature

1½ cups (180 g) powdered sugar

2 tbsp (11 g) Dutch-processed cocoa powder

Make the rich chocolate cake: Preheat the oven to 350°F (177°C). Spray the base and sides of an 8-inch (20-cm) round, 3-inch (7.5-cm)-deep cake pan with canola oil and line the base with parchment paper.

In a large saucepan, combine the butter, chocolate, brown sugar and cold water. Cook over medium-low heat, stirring, for 3 to 4 minutes, or until smooth. Remove from the heat and allow to cool for 15 minutes.

Add the eggs and whisk to combine. Add the all-purpose and self-rising flours and cocoa powder, and continue to whisk until well blended.

Transfer the batter to the prepared cake pan. Bake for 55 to 60 minutes, or until a skewer inserted into the middle of the cake comes out clean. Remove the cake from the oven. Set it aside for 10 minutes, then gently run a blunt knife around the edges to loosen the cake. Carefully turn it out onto a wire rack to cool completely.

Prepare the mint caramel shards, adding the mint at the stage when the bubbles subside. You will use the smaller shards for the frosting; reserve the larger shards for garnish.

Make the chocolate cream cheese frosting: Using a hand or electric mixer, beat together the cream cheese and butter until smooth and creamy. Add the powdered sugar, ½ cup (60 g) at a time, beating after each addition until smooth. Add the cocoa powder and beat till well blended.

Fold the smaller mint caramel shards into the frosting.

Assemble: Spread the chocolate mint frosting onto the top of the cooled cake. Decorate with the large mint caramel shards.

PINEAPPLE AND SAGE CAKE

Until a year ago, my fondness for sage was confined to a brown butter, pumpkin and sage pasta. Then, I happened to try it in a crumble, and I was completely awestruck by this aromatic herb. The earthy flavor of sage is difficult to replicate with other herbs. Sweet pineapple pairs wonderfully with it. To keep things easy and reduce the amount of preparation required, I used canned pineapple. You may certainly raise the quantity of sage according to how well versed you are with this herb.

Pineapple Topping

Canola oil spray, for pan

¼ cup (57 g) unsalted butter

½ cup (110 g) light or dark brown sugar

10 fresh sage leaves

5 or 6 canned pineapple rings

Pineapple and Sage Cake

⅔ cup (152 g) unsalted butter, at room temperature

1 cup (200 g) granulated sugar

3 large eggs

1½ cups (188 g) self-rising flour

½ cup (45 g) desiccated coconut

5 to 6 sage leaves, chopped finely

⅔ cup (160 ml) milk

Make the pineapple topping: Preheat the oven to 350°F (177°C). Spray the base and sides of an 8-inch (20-cm) round, 3-inch (7.5-cm)-deep cake pan with canola oil and line the base with parchment paper.

In a small saucepan, cook the butter and brown sugar together over low heat. Stir until the butter has melted and the mixture is smooth. Pour the mixture over the base of the prepared pan. Arrange the sage leaves and pineapple slices over the sugar mixture.

Make the pineapple and sage cake: In a large bowl, beat together the butter and granulated sugar until light and fluffy. Add the eggs, one at a time, beating well after each addition. Fold in the flour, desiccated coconut and sage leaves. Add the milk and mix until just combined.

Spread the batter over the pineapple topping in the prepared pan. Bake for 50 to 55 minutes, or until a skewer inserted into the middle of the cake comes out clean. Remove the pan from the oven. Set it aside for 10 minutes, then gently run a blunt knife around the edges to loosen the cake. Carefully turn it out onto a wire rack to cool.

FIZZY AND BOOZY CAKE-TAILS

Cake is fantastic. Even better are alcoholic cake infusions. While rum is a necessary component for a lot of holiday cakes and desserts, whiskey is a nice complement to cakes that are rich and creamy. There are, however, a variety of alternative methods to add a little alcohol to your cakes. Baking with alcohol is a great way of adding unique flavors and fragrances to a creation.

When including alcohol in your cakes, it's crucial to use alcoholic beverages that you genuinely love consuming. Consider your preferred wine or liqueur—a beverage you currently own and would be pleased to incorporate into your bake. Or, if you're feeling adventurous, go out and get something new.

When pairing alcohol with cakes, it's vital to consider the type of cake. Is it light and creamy, tart and fruity, or rich and chocolaty? Different types of alcohol will amplify these flavors differently.

STRAWBERRY MOJITO CAKE

Do you have a weakness for minty mojitos? Then you'll go crazy for this mojito cake, which is flavorful, light and fresh. The mint-lime combination truly shines in this recipe and gives it its refreshing overtones. Throw strawberries in the mix and you have an unforgettable dessert. The finishing touch is a zesty, sour cream glaze.

Strawberry Mojito Cake

Canola oil spray, for pan

1 cup + 2 tbsp (226 g) granulated sugar

½ cup (46 g) fresh mint leaves

1 tbsp (6 g) lime zest

1⅓ cups (166 g) all-purpose flour

1 tsp baking powder

2 tbsp (16 g) cornstarch

½ cup (114 g) unsalted butter, at room temperature

2 large eggs

⅓ cup (80 ml) sour cream

¼ cup (60 ml) milk

¼ cup (60 ml) fresh lime juice

2 tbsp (30 ml) rum

Sour Cream Icing

⅔ cup (79 g) powdered sugar

2 tbsp (30 ml) sour cream

1 tsp lime zest

For Garnish

8 to 10 fresh strawberries

Make the strawberry mojito cake: Preheat the oven to 350°F (177°C). Thoroughly spray the center and sides of an 8-inch (20-cm, 8-cup [1.9-L]) Bundt pan with canola oil.

In a food processor, process the granulated sugar, mint leaves and lime zest until the leaves are finely processed and the sugar looks green. Transfer 2 tablespoons (54 g) of the mint mixture to a shallow plate and reserve to use later for the minted strawberries.

In a separate bowl, stir together the flour, baking powder and cornstarch.

In a large bowl, beat together the butter and the remaining mint mixture until pale and fluffy. Add the eggs, one at a time, beating well after each addition. Fold in the flour mixture, alternating with the sour cream and milk. Add the lime juice and rum, and mix until just combined.

Transfer the batter to the prepared Bundt pan. Bake for 50 to 55 minutes, or until a skewer inserted into the middle of the cake comes out clean. Remove the cake from the oven. Set it aside for 5 minutes, then gently run a blunt knife around the edges and the center to loosen the cake. Carefully turn it out onto a wire rack to cool completely.

Make the sour cream icing: Into a small bowl, sift the powdered sugar. Add the sour cream and lime zest. Stir with a spoon until well combined.

Assemble: Once the cake has cooled completely, pour the icing over the sides and the top of the cake. Toss the strawberries in the reserved mint mixture and place on top of the cake.

NOTE: For mint lovers, candied mint (page 152) would make a fantastic garnish for this refreshing cake.

PEACH BELLINI CAKE

⇉ Makes a 7-inch (18-cm) round cake ⇇

The ultimate summer aperitif in the form of cake! You don't need a flute for this one, just some freshly pureed peaches and Prosecco. This cake has everything you might want for a birthday celebration, bachelorette party or wedding shower. The frosting gains a faint tang from the Prosecco, balancing out the richness of the cake.

Peach Cake

Canola oil spray, for pan

2 fresh peaches (about 8.5 oz [243 g]), pitted, chopped roughly

½ cup (120 ml) Prosecco

1 cup (125 g) self-rising flour

⅔ cup (83 g) all-purpose flour

1 tsp baking soda

½ cup (114 g) unsalted butter, at room temperature

1 cup (200 g) granulated sugar

2 large eggs

½ cup (120 ml) buttermilk

Prosecco Buttercream

½ cup (120 ml) Prosecco

½ cup (114 g) unsalted butter, at room temperature

2 cups (240 g) powdered sugar

1 tsp vanilla extract

1½ tbsp (22 ml) whole milk

For Garnish

1 peach, pitted and sliced thinly

Make the peach cake: Preheat the oven to 350°F (177°C). Spray the base and sides of a 7-inch (18-cm) round, 3-inch (7.5-cm)-deep cake pan with canola oil and line the base with parchment paper.

In a blender, combine the peaches and Prosecco and blend until the mixture turns into a smooth puree.

In a medium-sized bowl, combine the self-rising flour, all-purpose flour and baking soda.

In a large bowl, beat together the butter and granulated sugar until pale and fluffy. Add the eggs, one at a time, beating well after each addition.

Fold in the flour mixture, alternating with the peach puree and buttermilk.

Transfer the batter to the prepared cake pan. Bake for 60 to 65 minutes, or until a skewer inserted into the middle of the cake comes out clean. Remove the cake from the oven. Set it aside for 10 minutes, then gently run a blunt knife around the edges to loosen the cake. Carefully turn it out onto a wire rack to cool completely.

Make the Prosecco buttercream: In a small saucepan, bring the Prosecco to a boil over medium-high heat. Lower the heat to medium and let simmer until reduced to about 2 tablespoons (30 ml), 7 to 10 minutes. Remove from the heat and set aside to cool completely to room temperature.

In a large bowl, using an electric mixer, beat the butter until light and fluffy, 2 to 3 minutes. Add the powdered sugar, a little at a time, beating constantly until well combined, scraping down the sides of the bowl as and when required. Add the vanilla and milk, and beat until smooth.

Assemble: Place the cake on a cake stand or serving plate. Using a piping bag fitted with an open star nozzle, pipe a border of the buttercream onto the top of the cake. Decorate with fresh peach slices.

BOOZY TOFFEE APPLE RUM CAKE

⇒ Makes a 7-inch (18-cm) round cake ⇐

No cocktail shaker is required here, though it is inspired by my favorite apple daiquiri cocktail. Swapping lime with cinnamon makes it the perfect autumn cake, although a word of caution with the toffee apples. They are highly addictive!

Add a few black-tinted Meringue Kisses (page 156) and watch this spicy, boozy, fun cake become the star of your next Halloween party.

Boozy Apple Cake

Canola oil spray, for pan

⅔ cup (152 g) unsalted butter, at room temperature

¾ cup (150 g) granulated sugar

2 large eggs

1½ cups (188 g) self-rising flour

1 tsp ground cinnamon

1 tsp ground nutmeg

½ cup (120 ml) sour cream

2 tbsp (30 ml) rum

1 large apple, peeled, cored and chopped

Toffee Apples

4 medium apples

1 cup (200 g) granulated sugar

1 tbsp (21 g) liquid glucose or light corn syrup

1 tsp distilled white vinegar

¼ cup (60 ml) water

1 tbsp (15 ml) rum

2 or 3 drops red food coloring

Make the boozy apple cake: Preheat the oven to 350°F (177°C). Spray the base and sides of a 7-inch (18-cm) round, 3-inch (7.5-cm)-deep cake pan with canola oil and line the base with parchment paper.

In a large bowl, beat together the butter and granulated sugar until pale and fluffy. Add the eggs, one at a time, beating well after each addition.

Add the flour, cinnamon, nutmeg and sour cream, and continue to beat until just combined. Add the rum and mix well. Fold in the chopped apples.

Transfer the batter to the prepared cake pan. Bake for 55 to 60 minutes, or until a skewer inserted into the middle of the cake comes out clean. Remove the cake from the oven. Set it aside for 10 minutes, then gently run a blunt knife around the edges to loosen the cake. Carefully turn it out onto a wire rack to cool completely.

While the cake cools, make the toffee apples: Line a baking sheet with parchment paper. Wash the apples in hot water to remove any wax coating. Place them between paper towels to dry. Chill them in the fridge for about an hour, so that the toffee coating will set quickly on them. Push a wooden skewer or chopstick into the top of each apple. This will ensure easy dipping in and out of the toffee.

In a medium-sized saucepan, combine the granulated sugar, glucose, vinegar, water and rum. Cook over low heat, stirring frequently, until the sugar has dissolved, 3 to 4 minutes. Increase the heat to medium-high and bring to a boil. Cook without stirring for 15 to 20 minutes, or until the toffee reaches a hard crack stage (300°F [150°C] on a candy thermometer), brushing the sides of pan with a pastry brush dipped in water to prevent crystallization. If you are not using a thermometer, you could check whether the toffee has reached this stage by adding 1 teaspoon of the toffee to a glass of ice-cold water. If it sets hard immediately, it's ready.

Add the food coloring. Mix and allow the bubbles to subside slightly. Working quickly, dip an apple into the toffee, tilting the pan to coat. Allow the excess toffee to drain, then stand the apple on the prepared baking sheet. Repeat with the remaining apples. Let set for about 30 minutes, or until dry to the touch.

(continued)

Cinnamon Buttercream
½ cup (114 g) unsalted butter, at room temperature

2 cups (240 g) powdered sugar

1 tsp ground cinnamon

1½ tbsp (22 ml) whole milk

For Garnish (optional)
Sprinkles

Make the cinnamon buttercream: In a large bowl, using an electric mixer, beat the butter until light and fluffy, 2 to 3 minutes. Add the powdered sugar, a little at a time, beating constantly until well combined, scraping down the sides of the bowl as and when required. Add the cinnamon and milk, and beat until smooth.

Assemble: Place the cake on a cake stand or serving plate. Using a piping bag fitted with an open star nozzle, pipe the buttercream onto the top of the cake. Place the cooled and set toffee apples on the cake. Decorate with sprinkles, if desired.

ESPRESSO MARTINI BAVARIAN CAKE

⇒ Makes an 8-inch (20-cm) round cake ⇐

Skip the wait for the bartender to shake up this wildly popular cocktail. A luscious mousse and your favorite cocktail are combined into one insanely delicious Bavarian dessert that can be made at home without the hassle. For an extra coffee kick, whisk a teaspoon of instant coffee powder into the saucepan when the egg-milk mixture is being cooked. Meringue Kisses (page 156) are a great alternative to the whipped cream decoration.

Cookie Crust
Canola oil spray, for pan

7 oz (200 g) graham crackers or digestive biscuits

½ cup (114 g) unsalted butter, melted

Espresso Martini Bavarian Filling
5 tsp (16 g) powdered gelatin

2 tbsp (30 ml) water

4 large egg yolks

¾ cup (150 g) sugar

2 tbsp (16 g) cornstarch

½ cup (120 ml) whole milk

1 tsp vanilla extract

1½ cups (360 ml) heavy cream, divided

2 tbsp (30 ml) Kahlúa®

For Assembly
½ cup (120 ml) heavy cream, whipped to stiff peaks with 1 tbsp (15 ml) Kahlúa

1 tsp unsweetened cocoa powder, for dusting

Make the cookie crust: Spray the base and sides of an 8-inch (20-cm) round, 3-inch (7.5-cm)-deep springform pan with canola oil and line the base with parchment paper. In a food processor, process the graham crackers until they resemble fine crumbs. Add the butter and process briefly until combined. Press the mixture evenly over the base of the prepared pan. Chill in the fridge for 30 minutes.

Make the espresso martini Bavarian filling: In a small bowl, combine the gelatin and water. Set aside to bloom.

In a heavy-bottomed saucepan, combine the egg yolks, sugar, cornstarch, milk and vanilla, and whisk them together. The mixture will initially appear a bit dry, but will become smooth upon whisking. Add ½ cup (120 ml) of the cream and whisk until smooth.

Place the saucepan over low heat and cook, whisking constantly, until the mixture starts to thicken, 6 to 7 minutes. It is important to do this slowly and steadily so the eggs don't scramble and the cornstarch cooks evenly. The mixture is ready when it resembles custard and is thick enough to coat the back of a spoon.

Remove the saucepan from the heat. Add the gelatin mixture and Kahlúa. Mix until all the gelatin is dissolved. The heat from the custard should be enough to cook the gelatin. Strain the mixture into a large bowl. Set aside to cool to room temperature.

In a separate bowl, beat the remaining cup (240 ml) of cream into soft peaks. It should be thick enough to form soft shapes and just firm enough to hold briefly as you lift the whisk, then fall back into the cream. Fold the cream gently into the custard mixture until well combined.

Transfer the filling to the prepared pan over the cookie base. Chill in the fridge for a minimum of 4 hours, preferably overnight. When ready to serve, decorate with the Kahlúa-spiked whipped cream. Dust with cocoa powder. Slice and enjoy cold.

CHAI CHOCOLATE CAKE WITH RUM SAUCE

Makes a 10-inch (25-cm) Bundt cake

Have you ever wondered what Wednesday Addams's favorite cake might look like, if she had one? This sinfully spiced, dark adult cake is fit for our favorite ominous and macabre character. Whether you like the Addams family or not, you will feel guilty after eating this dangerously seductive Bundt cake, but in a good way. Oh, and the rum butter sauce—pure genius or pure wickedness, you decide!

Chai Chocolate Cake

Canola oil spray, for pan

1¾ cups (219 g) all-purpose flour

1¾ cups (350 g) granulated sugar

⅓ cup (40 g) Dutch-processed cocoa powder

2 tsp (9 g) baking soda

2 tsp (9 g) baking powder

1 tbsp (8 g) ground cinnamon

1½ tsp (3 g) ground ginger

1 tbsp (6 g) ground cardamom

1 tsp ground allspice

Pinch of salt

2 large eggs

1 cup (240 ml) buttermilk

½ cup (120 ml) vegetable oil

½ cup (120 ml) water, at room temperature

Rum Butter Sauce

½ cup (110 g) packed light or dark brown sugar

½ cup (114 g) unsalted butter, cubed

⅔ cup (160 ml) heavy cream

¼ cup (60 ml) rum

Make the chai chocolate cake: Preheat the oven to 350°F (177°C). Spray a 10-inch (25-cm, 12-cup [2.8-L]) Bundt pan well with canola oil.

In a large bowl, stir together the flour, granulated sugar, cocoa powder, baking soda, baking powder, cinnamon, ginger, cardamom, allspice and salt. Add the eggs, buttermilk, vegetable oil and water. Using an electric mixer, beat on medium-high speed for 2 minutes. The batter will be thin.

Pour the batter into the prepared pan. Bake for 55 to 60 minutes, or until a skewer inserted into the middle of the cake comes out clean. Remove the pan from the oven. Set it aside for 5 minutes, then gently run a blunt knife around the edges and the center to loosen the cake. Carefully turn it out onto a wire rack to cool completely.

Make the rum sauce: In a medium-sized saucepan, combine the brown sugar, butter, cream and rum. Cook over medium heat, stirring frequently, until the sauce starts to boil. Boil for a further 4 to 5 minutes, stirring frequently, until the sauce is slightly reduced and thickened. Remove from the heat, let cool and store in the refrigerator until needed. The sauce will thicken further upon cooling.

Assemble: Once the cake has cooled down, drizzle the cake with the rum butter sauce. The cake is best enjoyed warm or at room temperature.

FIG, WALNUT AND WHISKEY SEMIFREDDO

Makes an 8 × 4–inch (20 × 10–cm) loaf

The less popular sibling of the Italian gelato, a semifreddo has the consistency of a frozen mousse and is served by the slice. This one has roasted walnuts inside and is laced with figs that have been steeped in whiskey. The best part is that you don't need an ice-cream maker. If you don't mind the extra effort, decorate with Caramel Shards (page 159) to increase appeal. It's totally worth it!

1 cup (157 g) dried figs, sliced thinly

¼ cup (60 ml) whiskey

2 large eggs

4 large egg yolks

⅓ cup (67 g) sugar

1¾ cups (420 ml) heavy cream, whipped to almost stiff peaks

⅔ cup (77 g) walnuts, roasted and chopped, plus more for garnish

4 fresh figs (160 g), quartered, for garnish (optional)

It is best to prepare the figs the night before. In a small bowl, soak the figs in the whiskey. Cover the bowl and set aside for 3 to 4 hours, preferable overnight.

Line the base and sides of an 8 × 4–inch (20 × 10–cm), 3-inch (7.5-cm)-deep loaf pan with plastic wrap.

In a large heatproof bowl, combine the eggs, egg yolks and sugar. Place the bowl over a saucepan that is half–filled with simmering water over low heat. Whisk the egg mixture until thick and creamy, 4 to 5 minutes. Remove the bowl from the heat. Continue to whisk for another 5 minutes, or until the mixture cools to room temperature or barely lukewarm to touch.

Fold in the cream, fig mixture and roasted walnuts. Transfer to the prepared pan and freeze for a minimum of 6 hours. When ready to serve, decorate with fresh figs (if using) and extra walnuts. Slice and serve.

DRUNKEN HUMMINGBIRD CAKE

⇒ Makes a 9-inch (23-cm) round cake ⇐

Your favorite tropical piña colada cocktail is transformed into a delectable dessert with this "drunken" cake. Here, I've integrated some of the traditional hummingbird cake flavors—a delicious blend of bananas, pineapple, coconut, walnuts and cinnamon. What's not to love, right? It has a boozy finish on account of the Malibu® infusion, which will have you coming back for more.

Hummingbird Cake

Canola oil spray, for pan

2 cups (250 g) self-rising flour

½ cup (45 g) desiccated coconut

1¼ cups (275 g) light or dark brown sugar

1 tsp ground cinnamon

2 ripe bananas, mashed

2 large eggs, beaten lightly

¾ cup (180 ml) vegetable oil

16 oz (455 g) crushed pineapple, drained

¼ cup (60 ml) Malibu liqueur or coconut rum

½ cup (59 g) walnuts, chopped

Coconut Rum Buttercream

½ cup (114 g) unsalted butter, at room temperature

2 cups (240 g) powdered sugar

1 tbsp (15 ml) Malibu liqueur or coconut rum

1 tbsp (15 ml) coconut cream

For Assembly

4 or 5 dehydrated or fresh pineapple slices, for garnish

Make the hummingbird cake: Preheat the oven to 350°F (177°C). Spray the base and sides of a 9-inch (23-cm) round, 3-inch (7.5-cm)-deep cake pan with canola oil and line the base with parchment paper.

In a large bowl, combine the flour, coconut, brown sugar and cinnamon. Stir well to mix. Add the mashed bananas, eggs, vegetable oil, crushed pineapple and Malibu. Mix until well blended. Fold in the walnuts.

Transfer the batter to the prepared cake pan. Bake for 60 to 65 minutes, or until a skewer inserted into the middle of the cake comes out clean. Remove the cake from the oven. Set it aside for 10 minutes, then gently run a blunt knife around the edges to loosen the cake. Carefully turn it out onto a wire rack to cool completely.

Make the coconut rum buttercream: In a large bowl, using an electric mixer, beat the butter until light and fluffy, 2 to 3 minutes. Add the powdered sugar, a little at a time, beating constantly until well combined, scraping down the sides of the bowl as and when required. Add the Malibu and coconut cream, and beat until smooth.

Assemble: Place the cake on a cake stand or serving plate. Using an offset spatula or the back of a spoon, spread the buttercream onto the cake. Decorate with dehydrated or fresh pineapple slices.

RED WINE POACHED PEAR ALMOND CAKE

Do you really want to brag about your amazing cabernet sauvignon? To truly impress your guests, save it for the final course. Red wine and chocolate are generally the obvious choice, but for this cake, I opted to use the wine-poached pears in a nutty creation instead. Despite how elegant and opulent it looks, poached pears are the easiest topping to make.

Red Wine Poached Pears

1 cup (240 ml) red wine

¼ cup (50 g) sugar

1 stick cinnamon

2 whole star anise

1 strip orange peel (about 1" [2.5-cm] wide)

3 pears (528 g) peeled, halved, cores removed

Almond Cake

Canola oil spray, for pan

½ cup (114 g) unsalted butter, at room temperature

½ cup (100 g) sugar

3 large eggs, at room temperature

1 cup (125 g) self-rising flour

1 tsp ground cinnamon

½ cup (51 g) almond meal

¼ cup (60 ml) red wine sauce

½ cup (54 g) flaked almonds

Make the red wine poached pears: In a medium-sized saucepan, combine the wine, sugar, cinnamon, star anise and orange peel over medium heat. Cook, stirring, for 2 minutes, or until the sugar dissolves. Add the pears and bring to boil, making sure the pears are covered with the wine mixture. Lower the heat to low. Simmer, turning occasionally, for 25 to 30 minutes, or until the pears are tender and the sauce thickens slightly.

Remove from the heat. Transfer the mixture to a bowl and chill in the fridge for 6 hours, preferably overnight, for the color and flavors to develop. The color will deepen with time.

Make the almond cake: Preheat the oven to 350°F (177°C). Spray the base and sides of an 8-inch (20-cm) round, 3-inch (7.5-cm)-deep cake pan with canola oil and line the base with parchment paper.

In a large bowl, beat together the butter and sugar until pale and fluffy. Add the eggs, one at a time, beating well after each addition. Fold in the flour and cinnamon alternately with the almond meal, and stir in ¼ cup (60 ml) of the pears' wine sauce.

Pour the mixture into the prepared pan. Drain the poached pears, slice lengthwise and arrange, overlapping, in a circle, on top of the batter. Sprinkle with the flaked almonds. Bake for 50 to 60 minutes, or until a skewer inserted into the middle of the cake comes out clean. Remove the cake from the oven. Set it aside for 5 minutes, then carefully turn it onto a wire rack.

Enjoy warm or at room temperature.

CANDY LAND: DESSERT ACCESSORIES

We eat with our eyes. It has been uttered so frequently and for so long that it is now considered clichéd. However, it's true and is especially relevant when talking about cakes and dessert.

A cake's appearance can be radically changed by garnishes or accessories. The purpose of a garnish is multifold. Besides covering any defects or cracks in your cakes, if they have any, it also adds height, drama, color, and complementary flavor to the main cake. Garnishes not only add a touch of class and flair to your beautiful creation, but they can be delicious in their own right!

All the dessert accessories in this book use just three or four ingredients. They are quite simple to create, using basic techniques that work wonders, and can be prepared in bulk for prolonged usage.

When kept in an airtight container, Meringue Kisses (page 156), Marzipan Fruits (page 151), and Dehydrated Citrus (page 155) can last up to two weeks. Caramel Shards (page 159) are best stored layered with parchment paper in an airtight container at room temperature, in a cool, dry location, because they are a hard-cooked candy. It is best to make Candied Herbs (page 152) no more than two days in advance before utilizing them.

These cake accessories are adaptable in that one may experiment with different flavors and textures. For instance, caramel shards can be molded into the shape of hazelnuts or combined with a variety of nuts, seeds or herbs to create cake ornaments. Similarly, marzipan can be molded to resemble any fruit.

When it comes to using them in innovative ways, the possibilities are endless.

MARZIPAN FRUITS

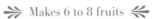 Makes 6 to 8 fruits

If you loved Play-Doh as a kid, this is your chance to embrace your inner child by creating a variety of fruits using marzipan. Marzipan is nothing but a ready-to-eat paste made of sugar and almonds, which means it's delicious. It can be used in a number of ways, but these adorable little fruits are a personal favorite. Marzipan fruits can decorate a variety of cakes, such as the Apple, Pear and Blueberry Cake (page 69) and the Rocky Road Ice Cream Cake (page 85), or to add a playful touch to any creation.

1 (7-oz [200-g]) log marzipan
1 tbsp (8 g) cornstarch
Gel food coloring of your choice
Whole cloves

These are best made the day before you are making the cake, so they have time to set and firm up. Cover your work surface to prevent staining.

To make blue marzipan apples and pears, for example, divide the marzipan into two portions. Dust your work surface and hands with cornstarch to prevent marzipan from sticking to the surface or your hands.

Take one of the pieces and knead in about one drop of blue gel coloring until evenly colored (this will be for the apples), then knead in two drops of blue gel coloring into the second portion (for the pears).

For the apples, divide the lighter blue log into three or four portions. Take one piece, roll it into a ball, press slightly on the top and insert a clove for the stem.

For the pears, take one piece from the darker blue portion and use your hands to roll it into a ball, then taper it at the end to shape like a pear. Insert a clove at the top for the stem.

Place all the molded fruits on a tray lined with parchment paper and let dry, about 24 hours. Store in an airtight container at room temperature until needed.

CANDIED HERBS

Yield varies

Candied herbs add a festive touch to your cakes because they almost sparkle from the sugar coating. Candied rosemary in particular always reminds me of Christmas. Some of the cakes that greatly benefit from candied herbs are the Rosemary Crusted Cranberry Cheesecake (page 121), Mango Cake with Basil Cream Cheese Swirl (page 70), Stone Fruit Cake (page 59) and Lemon Basil Meringue Cake (page 112).

¼ cup (30 g) powdered sugar

1 large egg white

Fresh herbs (e.g., rosemary sprigs, mint leaves, basil leaves)

Place a wire rack atop a parchment paper–lined baking sheet.

Spread the powdered sugar on a shallow plate. In a small bowl, lightly whisk the egg white until frothy.

Using a clean paintbrush, coat the herbs, one at a time, with the egg wash. Alternately dip the leaf/sprig into the egg wash allowing any extra to drip off. Then, place the herb in the plate of sugar, turning evenly to coat both sides.

Set the sugared herbs on the wire rack, spacing them apart. Allow the herbs to dry overnight, turning them once. Once they are completely dry, store them in an airtight container.

Candied herbs are best consumed within 2 to 3 days.

DEHYDRATED CITRUS

 Makes about 15 slices

These are different from candied citrus that are softer and have been cooked in sugar syrup. Dehydrated citrus is sturdier, with a long shelf life, and look classy perched on a cake. Use them as a garnish on the Lemon Raspberry Loaf (page 64), Caramel Poached Pear and Spiced White Chocolate Cake (page 78), Mandarin and Fennel Seed Cake (page 91) or the Rosemary Crusted Cranberry Cheesecake (page 121).

---

1 orange, washed, cut thinly into ¼" (6-mm) rounds

1 lemon, washed, cut thinly into ¼" (6-mm) rounds

1 lime, washed, cut thinly into ¼" (6-mm) rounds

Preheat the oven to 212°F (100°C). Place a wire rack atop a parchment paper–lined baking sheet.

Place the citrus slices in a single layer on the wire rack.

Bake for 3 to 4 hours, turning once at around the 1½-hour point, until the slices are dry and brittle to touch. Remove from the oven. Allow to cool and then store in an airtight container for up to two weeks.

NOTE: Alternatively, the citrus slices can be dried in an electric dehydrator according to the manufacturer's instructions.

MERINGUE KISSES

These melt-in-your-mouth treats make the prettiest of decorations. Depending on the occasion, color them and dress them to match your cake. A few cakes that look stunning with meringue kisses are Apple, Pear and Blueberry Cake (page 69), Red Velvet Cake with Raspberries (page 73), Berry Charlotte (page 82), Rosemary Crusted Cranberry Cheesecake (page 121) and Boozy Toffee Apple Rum Cake (page 135).

Canola oil spray, for pan

Gel food coloring of your choice

3 large egg whites

Pinch of cream of tartar (optional)

¾ cup (150 g) sugar

1 tsp vanilla extract

Preheat the oven to 212°F (100°C). Spray two large baking sheets with canola oil and line with parchment paper. Prepare two piping bags, one fitted with a star nozzle and the other fitted with a round nozzle. Dip the tip of a skewer into a bottle of gel food coloring and draw four or five stripes down the inner sides of each piping bag.

In a large clean, dry bowl, using an stand or hand mixer, beat the egg whites until they form soft peaks. Add the cream of tartar (if using) and gradually add the sugar, 1 tablespoon at a time, while beating constantly after each addition. Add the vanilla and continue to beat until all the sugar has dissolved and the meringue is thick and glossy.

Spoon half of the meringue into the piping bag fitted with the star nozzle. Spoon the other half into the bag with the round nozzle. Onto the prepared baking sheets, pipe meringue kisses 1¼ to 1½ inches (3 to 4 cm) in diameter, spacing them at least ¾ inch (2 cm) apart.

Bake for 40 to 45 minutes, or until the meringue kisses feel dry to touch. Turn off the oven, leave the door ajar and allow to cool inside the oven. Store in an airtight container for 4 to 5 days.

CARAMEL SHARDS
WITH TWO VARIATIONS

 Makes enough to decorate a 9-inch (23-cm) cake

Whether it is broken into shards, stretched into strands or used to coat nuts or fruit, caramel offers bakers endless hours of amusement and a touch of refinement when placed on a cake. Examples are the mint caramel shards that garnish the Rich Chocolate Cake (page 125) and the candied hazelnuts that adorn the Hazelnut and Coffee Cake (page 74). The Fig, Walnut and Whiskey Semifreddo (page 143) can also be turned into a showstopper with the addition of caramel shards.

For Herb, Nut or Seed Caramel Shards

¾ cup (150 g) sugar

¼ cup (60 ml) water

2 tbsp (4–6 g, depending on herb) chopped fresh herbs of your choice or (about 7 g) sliced nuts and/or seeds of your choice

For Candied Hazelnuts

15 to 20 hazelnuts, toasted in a 350°F (177°C) oven for 8 to 10 minutes, then cooled

¾ cup (150 g) sugar

¼ cup (60 ml) water

For the herb, nut or seed caramel shards: Line a baking sheet with parchment paper.

In a medium-sized saucepan, combine the sugar and water. Cook over low heat until the sugar dissolves. Increase the heat and bring the mixture to a boil. Boil without stirring until the mixture turns golden, about 6 to 7 minutes. Remove the saucepan from the heat and set aside for 2 minutes. Once the bubbles subside, add the chopped herbs or nuts or seeds.

Pour the caramel, in an even layer, onto the prepared pan. Once the caramel is firm to the touch and has cooled down completely (15 to 18 minutes), break it into large and small shards/pieces. You could do it use a knife or simply break it with your hands.

For the candied hazelnuts: Place a chopping board on the counter and a baking sheet on the floor below (to catch any sticky drips). Insert the tip of a skewer into each hazelnut.

Using the technique described above, make the caramel. Instead of adding the nuts to the caramel, dip a skewered hazelnut into the caramel. If a strand develops when you dip the hazelnut, the caramel is done. If not, give the caramel some more time to settle.

Each skewer's end should be carefully inserted under the chopping board, leaving the rest of the skewer and its hazelnut suspended in the air beyond the counter, then left to cool. The caramel strands may attach to each other, so take care to space them apart. Remove each hazelnut from the skewer with care.

Spread out the dried nuts on a parchment paper–lined baking sheet and place in a cool, dry location (do not cover). The candied hazelnuts are best used the same day they are made.

ACKNOWLEDGMENTS

There isn't a single day in my life that I don't thank God for all the wonderful people in my life, including my family, friends, followers and all the people behind this book.

I am really appreciative of my family's unwavering support and encouragement, their willingness to put up with my long hours of recipe testing and photography as well as my never-ending chatter about pastries. I appreciate their candid feedback and recent habit of having cake for every meal.

My husband, Subhro, deserves the biggest thanks for being my rock during all of my highs and lows, cleaning endless dishes, racing to the store whenever I ran out of eggs or butter and doing everything on an ongoing basis to make my life amazing.

My sweet boys, Advik and Aryan, my sous chefs, best friends, fervent supporters, biggest cheerleaders and my greatest critics. Your inputs have been beyond valuable!

My adorable dog Biscoff, who cheered me up, kept me company, put up with my flour and cocoa-stained clothes, and expressed disapproval at all the towering cakes.

My parents, for their blessings and joyful response to my book. My sister, Sangeeta, and my brother, Sid, for being such positive influences in my life since we were children. Sweets and desserts have always played a significant role in our lives, and I'm glad we still share the same excitement as we did back when we used to steal treats from the cupboard.

A big thank-you to my sweet sister-in-law, Lacy, for always being so supportive and responding to all of my concerns from the USA regarding ingredients.

To my mentor and inspiration, Coty Farquhar, who gave me the opportunity to be a part of the exquisite *Styling* magazine. You saw something that I couldn't see eight years ago. Thank you for your guidance and thoughtfulness through the years.

To my beautiful editor, Katherine; I could not have asked for a better person to hold my hand through this unfamiliar yet thrilling journey. Thank you for your patience, wisdom and encouragement in every interaction I've had with you.

Thank you to my publisher, William, and senior editor, Sarah, in believing in me and giving me the opportunity to share my story with the world. To Meg, Molly and the design team, thank you for your expertise and passion in creating this book.

Heartfelt thanks, my sweetheart Ekua, for taking care of my health and my heart, for being the ideal support system and shoulder to lean on. You bring so much positivity into my life.

Beautiful Jasmine who always allayed my worries, excitedly sampled my cakes and encouraged me to do better, I am grateful for your friendship.

To Tanya, Elke, Mansi and Amsha, for helping me reach this point in my life. You were willing to go above and beyond in supporting me in accomplishing my goals.

To all my friends and cousins who have been the greatest advocates of my work, near and far; you are too many to list but know that I appreciate your kindness and support.

To the entire team at Learnt, thank you for appreciating my cakes.

To all the people who follow my blog and my social channels, have made my cakes in your own homes, left me thoughtful comments and inspired me to work harder, I am indebted to you. Thank you for being beside me on this beautiful journey.

ABOUT THE AUTHOR

As an entrepreneur, recipe creator, photographer, social media influencer and author of the multi-award-winning Australian food blog Sugar Et Al, Sonali Ghosh juggles many different hats. What started out as a humble food blog rapidly gained popularity worldwide. Sonali thinks that more bakers are needed in the world to use cakes to convey kindness and love. Because sharing shows that you care!

Reputable agencies, such as PhotoCuisine in France and fashion brand VIDA in the USA, are commissioned to use photographs of her work. She has written for well-known publications, including Australia's *Styling* magazine and Germany's *Sweet Dreams,* and her recipes have been featured on the Huff Post, in *Vogue, Cosmopolitan, Better Homes and Gardens,* The Kitchn and more.

In 2018, her photographs were shortlisted for the prestigious Pink Lady Food Photographer of the Year competition, and she was also a finalist for the CommsCon Influencer of the Year Award, an event that celebrates the stars of the PR and communication industry in Australia.

She kept moving up the ladder of success when, in 2019, she received the Blogger of the Year award at the Fresh Awards, in recognition of her contribution to the fresh produce industry in Australia through promotion of "imperfect" fruits and vegetables. Her blog evolved into a lucrative business whereby her passion, business model and work ethic impressed the judges at the AusMumpreneur awards, winning her a national award for B2B Service Excellence. She launched Magic Baker, her second business, as an extension of Sugar Et Al to satisfy the rising demand for specialty bakeware.

Sonali has appeared in *Sunrise* on Channel 7 as well as in various newspapers. Her list of clients include such global brands as Nespresso®, Nutella®, KitchenAid®, Lanson Group, Maille, Baileys and Paramount Pictures, and the food businesses Australian Eggs, Coles, and Lucky Nuts and many more. Sonali considers her biggest achievement to be her ability to delight the patrons of a stylish café she temporarily owned, and to turn the business around with her distinctive "Native Australian High Tea" that celebrated bush food native to Australia in a chic high tea setting.

Sonali was born and raised in Kolkata, India, and now calls sunny Sydney her home, together with her husband, Subhro, twin boys A & A and puppy Biscoff.

INDEX